RICHIE —
Goon Luck !

MW01531674

Lean TCO
for Fat-Free Consumables

Minimizing Consumable Supply

Total Cost of Ownership

Tim O'Meara

"At the lowest Total Cost of Ownership possible, assure that
employees can immediately obtain ideally suited supply items."

Published by Lean Mechanics

Copyright © 2009 by Lean Mechanics

Lean Mechanics
205 Powell Place, Suite 234
Brentwood, TN 37027
(615)599-5759

TABLE OF CONTENTS

Acknowledgements

There are too many people to thank for Lean TCO to include them all here. The support of my wife Laura has been there since the beginning. From calling to get me up in time for classes at Purdue... to dealing with all of the late hours as I pursued my career and furthered my education... to the trials that a spouse has to deal with when married to an entrepreneur... she has been my business partner as well as my life partner.

I have learned so much from so many people I have worked with over the years that it would be impossible to give them all sufficient credit. Late in the process of developing Lean TCO, I was fortunate to spend considerable time working with a valued customer that has taken advantage of all we have to offer. To Mike, we've covered the North American Continent together. Thanks for the opportunities over the years... you have had a critical impact on what has become my life's work. To Greg, thanks for all you taught me about 5S. When it comes to organization, your focus, commitment, and enthusiasm has influenced this book. To Jandra, your purchasing disciplines are what allow you to carry so much responsibility so effectively. To Linda, your hands-on, get-it-done style is a great example for anyone in management. To Frederick, I can only hope that someday I will become as good at my trade as you are at yours.

To my mother and father, thanks for the inspiration and encouragement. You were always there when I needed you. To my sons Josh and Mack, thanks for giving a proud dad so much to fight for during the "lean" years.

Introduction

Procurement professionals and members of executive management are no longer looking at purchase prices as the primary source of cost information. Although difficult to measure, there is an increasing level of understanding that Total Cost of Ownership (TCO) is far more important than prices-paid when making strategic sourcing decisions. This book is written for procurement professionals, inventory management professionals, financial professionals, and executives who seek dramatic cost reductions through continuous improvement. This book is also written for those who seek enduring customer-supplier partnerships built upon a foundation of shared TCO benefits. I invite customers and their suppliers to openly share the strategies and techniques detailed in this book as they partner to improve mutual profitability.

I developed Lean TCO as a Lean Total Cost of Ownership Program for consumable supplies. While Lean TCO is a lean continuous improvement program, it is *not* another lean methodology. There are plenty of lean methodologies... such as Six Sigma... for organizations to select from and apply. Your organization may already be involved in highly effective lean-based continuous improvement initiatives. Regardless of which, if any, lean methodologies your organization utilizes, I provide the framework for applying lean principles to all processes related to consumable supplies. That framework includes a combination of *principles* and *tools*, all of which can be readily adapted to your own continuous improvement methods.

These Lean TCO principles and tools span all consumable supply processes, from how supply items are selected to how supply items are distributed and consumed. We will refer to your "Lean TCO Program" throughout this book. Your Lean TCO Program will address all selection, requisition, purchasing, receiving, stocking, distribution, consumption, and accounting processes. Your Lean TCO Program will also penetrate the full depth of the supply chain, accounting for every cost that is incurred as supply items travel through the channel from the manufacturer's shipping dock to your receiving dock.

Your Lean TCO Program will produce lean processes that achieve minimum TCO for the supply items your organization uses. I advocate the use of Six Sigma, so I provide an implementation framework that can follow the top-level Six Sigma DMAIC acronym (Define - Measure - Analyze - Improve - Control). This implementation framework can be used in one of the following three ways:

1. **Apply Lean TCO directly.** The framework can be followed by your organization without

the detailed application of Six Sigma methodology.

2. **Adapt Lean TCO to your existing Six Sigma methods.** If your organization applies the structure and tools of Six Sigma, they can be readily incorporated into your Lean TCO Program.

3. **Adapt Lean TCO to your other continuous improvement methods.** The framework can be easily adjusted to follow the format your employees currently use for improvement projects.

As a comprehensive program that affects the supply chain, the involvement of your suppliers is essential for maximum success. Your Total Cost of Ownership is not only affected by the price and performance contributions of your supplier base, but by the ways those suppliers interact with your organization. In order to drive TCO to the lowest possible levels, these interactions must occur through processes and relationships that are defined within the context of true strategic partnerships. For that reason, Lean TCO addresses the formation of strategic supplier partnerships in detail.

I encourage suppliers to bring Lean TCO to the attention of their customers. Suppliers that understand how challenges internal to their customer's facilities affect their own costs are better positioned to forge the types of strategic partnerships I encourage in this book. I do not advocate price-based partnerships, only partnerships that substantially drive down mutual costs to the degree that price reductions can occur while both partners achieve greater profitability.

When working outside of well structured partnerships, sellers often seek to increase both sales and margin and buyers often seek to reduce prices paid. Although they both have the same responsibility to their respective organizations - to improve the bottom line - there is a natural assumption that price reflects directly on the performance of the buyer and seller. The buyer's organization is pleased to see price reductions achieved by the buyer (price reductions are the most easily measured "accomplishments" of the buyer), and the seller's organization is pleased to see healthy margins produced by the seller (margin dollar increases are the most easily measured "accomplishments" of the seller). Industry recognized terms such as "price creep", where a seller wins business with bargain prices and then slowly attempts to raise prices to produce acceptable margin, define the lack of trust that buyers can have with sellers. Sellers will often complain about buyers who are putting their products out for quote after legitimately doing their best to provide value to that buyer. Even if the seller retains the business after the new round of quotes, a lack of trust can settle in if the seller feels that their efforts at providing value are not appreciated. If the seller drops their pricing in order to retain the business, the buyer can lose trust in the seller with the belief that they had been charging higher prices than they were ultimately willing to accept.

Many buyers and sellers will state that commodity items are just that... and they both make a career out of turning the quotation crank.

Similar to a dating scene, and sometimes carried out in the same smoke-filled venue, some are on the prowl and others are seeking more meaningful long-term relationships. One objective of this book is to clear the smoke from the room and provide the environment for buyers and sellers to build the latter, eliminating the likelihood that either returns to the dating scene in the future.

Significant savings are achieved when effective TCO analysis overcomes price as the primary driver for decision makers. Furthermore, truly dramatic savings can occur with the implementation of a TCO framework that impacts both internal and supply chain efficiencies through properly structured strategic supplier partnerships. By establishing a focus on Total Cost of Ownership, including all activities within the channel than can drive up prices paid, a systematic approach can be established that allows buyers and sellers to unite against mutual costs and achieve substantial bottom-line improvements that could never be accomplished independently.

Lean TCO focuses on Total Cost of Ownership for Indirect Spend, and more specifically, for Indirect Materials (consumable supplies). The principles in this book can be applied to any industry, from manufacturing to healthcare, to Hotel, Restaurant, and Institutional (HRI) organizations, and to government organizations. Those who apply the strategies and techniques discussed in this book will not only achieve lower costs, they will enjoy enduring supplier partnerships that bring real value to all stakeholders. Our objective for the readers of this book is straightforward:

"At the lowest Total Cost of Ownership
possible, assure that employees can immediately
obtain ideally suited supply items."

Although the statement of the objective is simple, achieving that
objective requires the rigorous application of what I define as
Selection to Consumption (S2C) solutions that impact how a supply
item is selected, how it moves through the supply chain and into a
facility for use, how it moves within the facility and into the hands of
the end-user, and how the supply chain is compensated for the service
it has provided.

The supply industry cannot independently bring the solution to
the customer. Large suppliers with business methods dating back
many decades have tried to adapt legacy business models to customers
rightly demanding TCO savings. Free freight, volume rebates, Vendor
Managed Inventory (VMI), inventory consignment, and other cost
saving concepts are offered to customers in well-meaning attempts to
help reduce costs. The unfortunate reality is that these cost saving
ideas, when implemented outside of partnership-driven analysis, can
obscure the root causes of excessive cost and restrict the ability of
customers to achieve truly substantial TCO savings. If these and other
existing concepts could simply be combined to provide the ideal
solution for all customers, that ideal solution would already be widely
adopted.

I provide specific methods and tools that allow customers and suppliers to work together and achieve substantial, measurable results. I also provide the methods and tools that not only secure those gains but allow further gains to be accomplished through continuous improvement.

The majority of this book is written from the perspective of the customer. Not only can customers use this book to coordinate TCO reduction efforts with suppliers, suppliers can use this book to bring substantial value to their existing and prospective customers.

My hope is that you will not only read this book and apply much of what you learn, but that you will launch a formal Lean TCO Program that follows the guidelines provided. Furthermore, I hope that you encourage your key suppliers to read this book and become directly involved in your efforts as you move from supplier relationships to strategic supplier partnerships. Some customers will need to make changes to their supplier base, and perhaps even use this book to support supplier consolidation efforts, but we encourage you to consider your strong supplier relationships as potential strategic partnerships. With that in mind, we encourage you to get them fully involved in your Lean TCO Program.

You can expect to achieve substantial cost reductions by applying the principles presented here. You will start seeing those cost reductions quickly with the implementation of the tools presented in Chapter 2, Low Hanging Fruit. Your cost savings will accelerate as we dig deep into your supply related processes across all supply categories, driving TCO to the lowest possible levels.

No TCO reduction effort can be effective without attacking the excessive costs induced by supply item movement within the channel. I provide a detailed look at the ideal customer-supplier partnership and lay the groundwork for building those partnerships with a view towards reducing supply chain costs. I also sound caution on procurement contracts and provide some guidelines for contracts that can foster, rather than inhibit, ongoing TCO reduction within the strategic partnership.

This book centers on what I call the Lean TCO Triangle; the key interdependencies between items, processes, and suppliers that produce substantial challenge along with substantial opportunity for savings. I address the full spectrum of supply inventory management alternatives and corresponding vendor services. The use of visual tools for managing inventory is covered in detail; visual tools offer cost effective alternatives to transaction-based inventory control.

I conclude with considerations for multiple-facility organizations, addressing the significant challenges that large organizations face when attempting to standardize supply items and control expenses across multiple locations.

Chapter 1

Launching Your Lean TCO Program

Improvement projects don't get started with a formal proposal or the creation of a project team. They get started through a common awareness of a need to solve a problem or capture an opportunity. At the time of launch, all improvement projects have one or both of the following characteristics: a *visible* likelihood to either *increase revenues* or *decrease costs*. Lean Total Cost of Ownership (Lean TCO) is a cost reduction program that has resulted from my broad 25 year background in lean methodology and my more recent experience as a supplier to general industry. I have seen common practices across a diverse customer base that can dramatically escalate costs for relatively inexpensive consumable supplies. Lean TCO is a structured collection of the tools and techniques I have employed to help those customers drive down consumable supply expenses.

Supply related costs are everywhere you look, as if they are hiding in plain sight. The challenge is to bring these costs into the field of vision of the appropriate members of management. Some supply related overhead is buried so deep within an organization that it is hard to drag it out into the light of day. Employees involved with your internal supply related processes most likely have other primary job responsibilities. A safety coordinator might be the buyer of safety supplies. A member of the accounting staff that processes invoices for supply items might have other more demanding accounting responsibilities. Production supervisors who focus on daily production output might also specify supply items for their production areas.

Supply related processes are often random and uncontrolled, leading to an excessive number of supply items, supply item sources, and supply item purchases. Suppliers may stream in and out of offices and receiving areas so frequently that their presence goes unnoticed. Stocking areas may become so overrun with excess and obsolete inventory that employees have learned to accept searching the shelving to find the item they need. Ask some "what if" questions:

- What if you had a list of standard supply items?

- What if you decreased the number of Purchase Orders you place?

- What if needed supply items were always on hand?

- What if you had well organized supply inventory?

- What if you reduced the number of different supply items you buy?

If your organization is aware of excessive supply related costs, you are ready to communicate the opportunity for substantial cost reduction. Get some rough numbers on annual indirect material spend and discuss the potential of reducing TCO by 25% or more. To estimate your current TCO, you can conservatively add 50% to your annual spend for overhead costs; your organization could reasonably save 25% of that number:

Annual Spend	Total Cost of Ownership	Potential Savings
$100,000	$150,000	$37,500
$500,000	$750,000	$187,500
$10,000,000	$15,000,000	$3,750,000

Needless to say, the potential TCO savings your organization can achieve will be a function of the degree of control, the operational efficiencies, and the strategic supplier partnerships you currently have in place.

This book will give your Lean TCO Program a jump start if your organization already applies Six Sigma methods. If not, there is no need for concern. Following the DMAIC acronym will still provide your Lean TCO Program with a healthy top-level structure:

Define: Document the Current Condition and identify the objectives of the project.

Measure: Obtain the baseline performance of existing processes, including impact on costs.

Analyze: Study current processes to understand their operation and effects.

Improve: Modify, eliminate, and add processes as necessary to achieve the objectives of the project.

Control: Implement methods to assure the improvements continue to produce the desired results.

We will not get into the more complex tools that are a part of Six Sigma methods... there are plenty of books and consultants that can provide you with everything you could want to know... but we encourage you to apply Six Sigma to the fullest extent if it has been implemented at your organization.

Understanding Total Cost of Ownership

Total Cost of Ownership (TCO) is now a commonly used term that refers to the sum of all costs associated with an acquired item or service, including purchase price, cost of use, and overhead. TCO analysis can be applied to the purchase of everything from office supplies to office buildings, so it is important to clearly communicate how TCO will be defined with respect to consumable supplies. A clear definition of "consumables" also justifies some brief attention.

Consumables are items that are purchased on a repeat basis due to the fact that they are "consumed" during use by employees, machines, or equipment. Work gloves and printer cartridges are good examples. If a supply item must be purchased more than once per year, I recommend it be included in your Lean TCO Program. Examples of consumable supply categories include industrial, safety, office, MRO (Maintenance, Repair, and Operations), first aid, medical, food service, and janitorial. If a production process requires a power tool with an accessory, such as a grinder with a grinding disc, the accessory item would be considered a consumable. The power tool would not be considered a consumable unless it needed to be replaced regularly. I define Total Cost of Ownership for consumable supplies as all Selection to Consumption (S2C) costs.

The supply chain performs a series of actions for a sourced item that includes transporting the item as it travels through various channels between the manufacturing facility and the end-customer's facility. Total Cost of Ownership includes all supply chain activity, even if much of that cost is rolled into the purchase price for the item. The path through the supply chain that the item must follow has significant TCO ramifications.

A number of expenses are incurred when the item arrives at the customer's facility. With traditional methods, the item must be received and stocked, a packing list must be processed, an invoice must be processed, and a supplier must be paid. Performing these tasks can involve additional costs when backorders and shipping errors occur. The end-user of the item must then access the item in order to put it to use. These internal processes also have significant TCO ramifications.

For the purposes of this book, the definition of Total Cost of Ownership includes all internal and supply chain costs incurred from the time an item is specified until the time it is consumed by the end-user. While prices paid is a component of TCO, this book explores all costs that may be rolled into purchase prices in order to assure that customers and suppliers have the opportunity to impact those costs.

Involve Suppliers Early

When launching your Lean TCO Program, let your suppliers know immediately. Explain that you are initiating an effort to reduce Total Cost of Ownership and that you will be asking them to become involved. Ask for initial feedback on what they might gain if your supply inventory was under solid control and fewer but larger Purchase Orders were placed. Find out what ideas they might have from any of their own efforts to help reduce their customer's costs. Encourage your suppliers to look at their internal processes and understand how they impact your own processes.

Most suppliers are anxious to demonstrate value to their customer base. Most are continuously looking for ways to build stronger relationships and expand their business with their existing accounts. They have substantial investments in their customer base, not only with a history of providing service, but with considerable sales and marketing expenses incurred to land and maintain those business relationships. Furthermore, taking action to secure and grow an existing account is far less expensive than taking action to land a new account.

You are likely to find that most suppliers will welcome your questions and will express an eagerness to become involved in your improvement program. The more interested you are in controlling your costs, the more likely they are to benefit in the process. Would a supplier rather receive ten $250 orders or one $2500 order in the same time period? Talk with them about order consolidation and they will listen intently. They are also likely to be able to share what other customers have done to reduce order frequency.

Virtually all suppliers will like to hear that a customer is planning on building strategic partnerships with their supplier base. Some may feel a little threatened if their service levels or capabilities are lacking, but that is OK if it motivates them to elevate their performance. After you have launched your Lean TCO Program, the suppliers you have already spoken with will be ready to join in.

Suppliers: Share Your Own Internal Improvements

Nothing could be more encouraging to a customer's Lean TCO Program team than a supplier that can share in their efforts at reducing their own internal costs. As you establish strategic partnerships with your customers, you need to adapt your processes and services in a manner that provides benefit to those customers as well as your own operations. We do not advocate offering operationally expensive services without first working with your customer to integrate and streamline processes for maximum mutual benefit. Later in this book, we encourage customers to avoid cost diversion and focus on cost control... working with suppliers to drive down mutual costs... so be prepared to openly discuss your costs and your strategies to reduce them.

If your customer has read this book, they should be anxious to hear of any past or current continuous improvement efforts you have undertaken. Just as I recommend for customers, I recommend suppliers also apply lean methodology. Whether or not you are already a Six Sigma organization, you can use the DMAIC Six Sigma acronym as a roadmap for your improvement work. This is particularly important if your customers apply Six Sigma methodology as they will better understand the structure of your internal efforts. It will also be much easier to integrate improvement efforts between your organizations where appropriate.

The Lean TCO Program Definition

Your organization decides that too much manpower is being spent on ordering, receiving, and stocking consumable supply items. A team is formed and a project is launched with the objective of minimizing those expenses. In terms of solutions offered by the supply industry, what is the likely result of that project? Vendor Managed Inventory (VMI), where most otherwise internal functions are outsourced to suppliers. The team is able to present astonishing results: "Our annual payroll costs associated with ordering, receiving, and stocking supplies have gone from $354,000 to zero. The team has accomplished a 100% reduction in those expenses!" Is it possible that the team would actually raise, rather than lower, TCO with their VMI solution? Certainly. Even if they could successfully lower TCO, is it possible that they would mitigate the opportunity for substantially greater TCO savings? Absolutely.

Imagine another project team that is chartered to maximize performance-to-price ratios for a group of supply items. Perhaps this team learns that they can reduce expenses as a function of prices paid by changing to supply items that cost an average of 20% more but have double the average life. Is it possible that this team would actually raise, rather than lower, TCO with their new supply items? Certainly. Even if they could successfully lower TCO, is it possible that they would mitigate the opportunity for substantially greater TCO savings? Absolutely.

Some might suggest that the Lean TCO Program should be broken down into individual projects... but imagine the disagreements that could be raised between the two project teams above. One of many potential dilemmas is that the first project team has eliminated internal expenses through a supplier that doesn't offer the supply items the second team is selecting. As presented in Chapter 8, the Lean TCO Triangle shows the interdependence between your supply items, your suppliers, and your Selection to Consumption (S2C) processes. Chapter 9 addresses your S2C processes in detail.

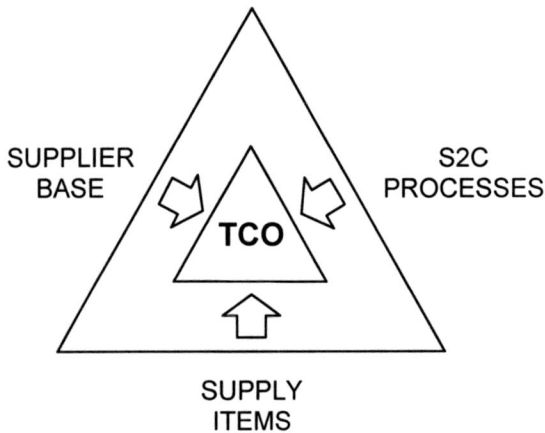

```
                    /\
                   /  \
                  /    \
                 /      \
                /        \
   SUPPLIER    /   /\     \   S2C
   BASE       / ⟨  TCO ⟩   \  PROCESSES
             /   /    \     \
            /   /  ⇧   \     \
           /_____\
              SUPPLY
              ITEMS
```

There is no sugar-coating the complexity of this effort. I can, though, assure you that the challenge of the hard work you are entering into will bring tremendous gains. As you build your Lean TCO Program team, be sure to involve representation for all stakeholders… for all departments that will be affected by the team's work. Those representatives can then work within the program to help assure that the overall team is making the best collective decisions possible.

A clear definition of your Lean TCO Program is essential to success. The definition of your program should compel management, your team members, and other stakeholders to take action. Most organizations have an opportunity to achieve such substantial savings through Lean TCO that the definition stage of the program will generate not only support but excitement. The definition should not simply state that there will be some savings through some process adjustments, it must communicate the breakthrough level of change that you are about to undertake. Consistent with Six Sigma methodology, our Lean TCO Program definition will include a Current Condition Statement and an Objective Statement.

The Current Condition Statement is a concise statement that addresses how your organization is currently procuring and managing supply inventory along with some key metrics. I recommend the following be included:

1. Estimated annual spend on supply items. Include all supply categories that will be covered by the Lean TCO Program (industrial, safety, office, and so on).

2. The number of current approved suppliers for the supply categories identified above.

3. Onsite services, if any, currently provided by those suppliers.

4. The number of Purchase Orders issued annually to those suppliers.

5. The methods used by employees to requisition and obtain supply items.

6. How new supply items are specified.

7. Current supply item inventory control methods.

8. The estimated total annual manpower spent in requisitioning, quoting, purchasing, receiving, stocking, distributing, and paying for supply items.

The resulting Current Condition Statement could read something like:

"We were invoiced $727,231 for industrial, safety, MRO, janitorial, and office supply items in the last fiscal year through a total of 23 different suppliers. In some cases, the invoice amounts include freight or delivery charges. We issued 291 Purchase Orders. Of the 23 suppliers, 3 provide on-site services including equipment inspections, stocking of first aid cabinets, and stocking of fasteners for the Maintenance Department. We have 4 primary internal locations for various supplies and employees will go to those locations to obtain what they need. Our tool crib is the only stocking location where we have an attendant on staff. We do not have a standard list of all supply items and new supply items can be selected by any employee that has a need. Employees submit requisitions to their Supervisors for approval who then forward approved requisitions to the Purchasing department. The estimated total manpower expended on supply related activity amounts to 5.2 employees annually (from requisition through vendor payment). Using a blended burdened rate of $34.00 per hour, our annual supply-related overhead is currently estimated to be $368,000.00. This brings our estimated annual Total Cost of Ownership for supply items to $1,095,000.00 excluding negligible inventory carrying costs."

If your organization does not have this level of information available, it is acceptable to make estimates as long as the basis of those estimates is logical and properly documented. The most critical part of creating the Current Condition Statement is to establish a top-level understanding of general practices and corresponding costs.

At this stage, don't worry about detailed processes and data. A closer look at your internal processes and data will occur during the next phase of the Lean TCO Program. If your detailed work in the next phase reveals changes to the preliminary information you gathered, it is perfectly acceptable to make updates to the Current Condition Statement based upon the new information.

After defining the Current Condition, you are in a position to consider what possible improvements could be achieved and the potential financial benefits. Similar to your work in preparing the Current Condition Statement, your work in preparing an Objective

Statement will involve some common sense estimates that can be updated during the next phase of the Lean TCO Program.

Where do you see opportunity for improvements with respect to processes, items, and suppliers? How much time is being invested in processes, and does that time appear reasonable? Does the breadth of your supplier base appear reasonable? How about the number of supply items currently in use? Referring back to our Current Condition Statement, we will work through some examples of how to establish some improvement objectives.

Starting with items, we determined in our example that there was no standard list of the supply items in use. Consider the supply item categories that will be a part of your project and assess the potential impact of standardization. Interview employees who use supply items and get a sense of how much variance exists in the supplies they are provided with. You could ask a production worker about the gloves they use. Is there more than one type of glove used by the worker? If so, is there a good reason? In a given work area, do all workers use the same type of glove? If you were looking at office supplies, you could determine how many unique types of office printers are in use and how that affects the number of ink cartridges that are required. Also ask employees how suitable the supply items are within their applications. Are they effective? Are they durable? Are they costly?

After some research, you should be able to generate a sense of the potential reduction in supply items. Look at various items within various categories and then extrapolate your findings to all supply items in use. Is a 10% reduction potentially possible but conservative? Is a 40% reduction potentially possible but optimistic? It might then be reasonable to select 25% as your initial target reduction. You should also be able to develop a sense of how effectively supply items have been selected based upon their application. If supply item selection has been somewhat random, you might anticipate some additional cost reduction from a rigorous supply evaluation effort. If employees commonly say "I just use what they give me and the supplies are always changing", you can expect even more substantial benefit from supply evaluation work.

Remember, you will communicate that your initial targets are rough estimates and that they will be adjusted in the next phase of the project as necessary.

Moving on to processes... Are they documented? Are they followed? Is there substantial process variance? If so, in what areas? We will continue with our premise that there is no standard list of supply items in place and that there is significant process variance as a result. How does the lack of a standard supply list impact processes? How is the time required to select and source supply items affected? How does this relate to the size and frequency of Purchase Orders and corresponding overhead costs? Again, talk to employees that are involved in supply related processes. What are their views of process variance and process efficiency? Extrapolate your estimates to all processes. Is a 40% improvement in process efficiency reasonable?

Finally, look at your supplier base. How many suppliers are there for each major supply item category? How many suppliers are providing products across multiple categories? For suppliers providing on-site services, are those services being performed productively and at an appropriate cost? Could those services be performed by internal personnel at considerably less expense? Would a 20% reduction in the number of suppliers be reasonable? If you are not in the Purchasing Department, be certain to include them in this preliminary assessment and to assure them that they will be directly involved in any sourcing considerations associated with the Lean TCO Program.

The corresponding Objective Statement could look something like this:

> "In order to produce a rough estimate of the potential value of the Lean TCO Program, we looked at a sample of items, processes, and suppliers in order to make some preliminary assessments. We are targeting a 20% reduction in the number of suppliers we currently use based upon the determination that we have more than one supplier for a number of supply categories. We anticipate considerable savings in prices paid through the implementation of a standard supply item list that will be developed through supply item performance evaluations where appropriate. We expect a 25% reduction in the number of unique supply items in use. Our accounting processes are performed consistently but we experience substantial process variance in other areas. We expect that a 40% improvement in process efficiency is achievable.

> We use supplier services in 3 areas and anticipate
> that work can be performed by internal personnel at
> a lower total cost. We are anticipating an estimated
> $350,000.00 in annual Total Cost of Ownership
> savings, a 32% reduction from an estimated TCO of
> $1,095,000.00 during the last fiscal year."

Even though these estimates are rough, which you have acknowledged in the Objective Statement, you are able to confirm they are reasonable based upon your preliminary work. More importantly, management has the ability to assess the potential value of the program based upon your projections and your supporting assumptions.

The Lean TCO Program Team

After completing the definition of your project, it is time to identify your team leader and pull together your proposed team members. You will want to involve team members that work within all affected parts of the organization. You will not only gather better information, you will have an increased likelihood that the team will generate buy-in and achieve superior results.

The most critical requirement of the team leader is that they have team leadership training. In Six Sigma organizations, this could be a Green Belt (or perhaps even a Black Belt if the organization assigns projects directly to Black Belts). A well-trained team leader with supply related responsibilities would be the natural choice.

Do not underestimate the importance of assembling the right team. Each team member will be entrusted with important responsibilities and each can have a substantial impact on overall team success. For this reason, I will begin by discussing key characteristics of ideal team members.

1. **Solid experience in their area of responsibility.** Without solid experience, the team member will be less effective at assessing data and feedback. They will also be less effective at recognizing key factors that will affect key program outcomes.

2. **Demonstrated flexibility.** No matter how experienced, those that say "but we have always done it this way" are not likely to be effective team members. Resistance to change will be enough of a challenge within the organization; it has no place within the Lean TCO Program team.

3. **Past improvement project experience.** Past success in any form of an improvement project will increase the team member's ability to contribute and envision positive results.

4. **Appropriate communication skills.** Notice that I say "appropriate" and not "good." The ability to gather and communicate information corresponding to their role on the team is what counts, not eloquence or public speaking skills.

5. **Respect from co-workers.** It is far more important that a team member be respected by co-workers than by management. The team will be gathering information from co-workers and will be seeking to impact some part of how co-workers will be performing their jobs. Respect is invaluable when it comes to getting good information and implementing change.

All team members may not meet all of these requirements. Your objective is to assemble the best team you can to produce the best results possible.

The team must include representation from those who specify, use, purchase, handle, and pay for supply items. Ideally, the team would also include someone in a finance role to assist with gathering and analyzing financial data, and someone in an Information Technology role that can assist with data communication.

Regarding your Finance Department, I have learned that many organizations struggle to accurately capture supply related costs. Even though Cost Accounts are commonly used, they are commonly used inaccurately. This can result in a challenge to obtain accurate financial data. A team member from your Finance Department could be a substantial asset in this area. I have also learned that Finance Departments are often frustrated by the inability to track supply related costs. They are aware of substantial indirect material spend, but they can have difficulty getting accurate information on that spend. It is likely that your Finance Department will gladly provide a team member if they view supply expenses as an area that needs cost reduction and cost control.

With the team members selected, responsibilities must be assigned so that each team member has a clear understanding of their role within the Lean TCO Program. I encourage the team leader to meet with each team member to agree upon a written statement of their responsibilities to the team.

I have had extensive team experience, from direct involvement on improvement teams to structuring teams as a member of executive management. As the head of an Engineering Department for a division of a multi-billion dollar corporation, I worked with Fred, a talented Engineer that was new to the idea of teams. I asked Fred to lead some of the new product development teams on behalf of our department and his own project work. He taught me an important lesson as he took on this new responsibility.

At first, Fred was resistant. He had over 30 years of product design experience and he stated that each employee in the corporation had their own area of expertise. He accurately expressed that their real value to the organization was based upon their individual skills and experience. He would become frustrated when, for example, a team member representing the Quality Department would challenge a team member representing the Sales and Marketing Department by saying their that their ideas related to a marketing effort should be adopted by the team. He felt that each team member should be respected for their own expertise, that they should hear thoughts and ideas from others with an open mind, and then get to the work that they were hired to do without resistance from the other team members.

Fred would not allow his team meetings to spiral into arguments between team members. Admittedly, I was at first concerned that Fred would limit open communication and the flow of ideas. What I learned from watching Fred's success was that his team members were actually more open to sharing their ideas because arguments were rare. Fred's teams operated with the clear understanding that accountability landed first with each team member's area of responsibility, and then with himself as the team leader. His teams were more productive, more likely to meet deadlines, and more likely to reach goals. They were also more likely to come up with new ideas that would challenge conventional thinking… in large part due to the respect granted to team members that may have to begin thinking in new ways.

The best way to assure an individual will not adapt to change is to tell that individual that you know better and as a result they must change. The most hardened "we've always done it this way" employees are far more likely to embrace change if they are respected for their knowledge and experience and given some ownership in determining what type of change should occur.

The lessons I learned from Fred were significant and I have carried them with me ever since. When you assemble your team, follow a meeting outline, share ideas, and get down to action items assigned to the members of your team according to their knowledge and experience. Curtail unproductive conversation and do not let the expression of strong opinions turn into destructive arguments.

Speaking of action items, do not leave team meetings without agreement from the team members that their action items and deadlines are acceptable and clearly understood. Encourage each team member to be respectful of the team and to demonstrate that respect by completing their action items on time.

Acknowledging the skills and experience of your team members will help your team avoid the common pitfall of pursuing change for the sake of change. A team member with strong resistance to a particular idea may well have knowledge and experience that justifies that resistance. Claiming that the team member does not have an open mind will not only frustrate that team member, it could cause the rest of the team to push for a direction they shouldn't. It is the job of the team to assure that all input is weighed and considered in a manner that produces the best results possible, and individual team member expertise and experience is an important consideration in that process.

Forget that overused "there's no *I* in *TEAM*" slogan… your team is a group of *I*ndividuals with *I*ndividual knowledge, *I*ndividual experience, *I*ndividual responsibilities, and *I*ndividual ideas that must be blended together for maximum benefit. If you disagree, consider what would happen if a professional sports team had every player change their positions. Running backs generally don't make good field goal kickers, and defensive lineman generally don't make good quarterbacks. I argue that an outstanding *TEAM* is comprised of outstanding *I*ndividuals that know how to work together.

Chapter 2

Low Hanging Fruit

"Low hanging fruit" can be defined as improvement opportunities that organizations should just "reach up and grab" rather than analyze. These types of opportunities involve readily apparent needs and readily apparent solutions. The good news is that you can make substantial progress in your Lean TCO Program with three areas of low hanging fruit:

- Gaining control of supply item selection
- Generating a Supply Item Master List
- Getting inventory organized

You will be facing some complex challenges when you begin detailed process analysis and improvement, but for now, were just going to grab some fruit.

Gain Control of Supply Item Selection

Stop the bleeding first. Most organizations have a wide group of employees in a wide variety of job positions that can specify supply items. In some cases, any employee that needs a supply item can search through catalogs or online and specify an item for purchase. As I discussed early in this book, uncontrolled selection and purchase of supply items can lead to duplicate effort, an excessive number of unique supply items, and an excessive number of suppliers. It can also lead to excessive purchasing, receiving, and supplier payment overhead expense... it can lead to excessive Total Cost of Ownership.

In some cases, an employee will specify an item that had been purchased previously. The time spent in selecting the item becomes duplicated effort. There is also the risk that the employee will select a different version of the item from a new supplier, incurring the cost of having the new supplier set up in the organization's accounting system.

I had the privilege of working with Greg, a true 5S expert, while implementing Lean TCO at his facility. Greg and I worked closely together to improve the control of supply items in their tool crib. Greg was well underway in the implementation of 5S organizational improvements within the tool crib when I was brought into his improvement project.

As with many facilities, not all supply items were specified and Production Supervisors often had to submit Purchase Requisitions for items they needed in their departments. Greg and I were discussing how extension cords should become a tool crib item since they were commonly requisitioned by the production staff. When Greg was explaining the benefits of specification and standardization to a member of their finance team, he posed this question:

> "If we asked ten Production Supervisors to select
> and requisition extension cords, how many different
> types of extension cords would we end up
> purchasing?"

The member of the finance team accurately estimated:

> "Ten."

The degree of specification and standardization of the supply items a facility uses is directly proportional to the degree of TCO savings that a facility can achieve. To say it another way, specification and standardization is the foundation of a TCO reduction effort.

Let's consider the TCO components of an extension cord requisitioned by, purchased for, and delivered to a Production Supervisor. We will assume that the purchase price of the extension cord is $10 and compare the purchase price to the corresponding overhead associated with the purchase.

We will make some conservative assumptions in estimating these overhead costs:

Time spent by the Production Supervisor selecting the extension cord and submitting a Purchase Requisition	15 min
Time spent by a Manager to review and approve the Purchase Requisition	10 min
Time spent by the Purchasing Agent to place a Purchase Order	10 min
Time spent by receiving personnel to receive the shipment	10 min
Time spent by stock room personnel to deliver the extension cord to the Production Supervisor	10 min
Time spent by the Accounting Department to receive, file, pull, and match the supplier invoice to the packing list	15 min
Time spent by the Accounting Department to process payment	15 min
Total:	**85 min**

Assuming an average burdened rate of $30 per hour, the total cost of the time spent by internal personnel would be approximately $42 or 420% of the amount of the purchase. Our cost estimate is substantially below the commonly quoted estimate of $150 for the cost of an organization to process a Purchase Order. It also does not account for any freight or delivery charge. Although our example is overly simplistic and somewhat exaggerated by a low-dollar purchase, it does demonstrate how internal overhead costs can sometimes become a multiple of prices paid. Small and frequent Purchase Orders are common in most organizations; consider the relative value of a specified extension cord, purchased in combination with other products from a given supplier, and readily available in a stocking area.

Also of interest from a TCO perspective would be the events leading up to the Production Supervisor making the requisition for the extension cord, including time spent by a production worker trying to locate an extension cord and any work stoppage costs due to the un-powered device awaiting the cord. Work stoppages that result from a lack of supply item availability are the single largest component of TCO.

One quick story related to item standardization. I was at a customer's facility working on reducing TCO for safety and industrial supplies. The corporate head of Environmental, Health, and Safety was also at the facility. He had mentioned to me that he needed to add another item to their list of respiratory protection products. I expressed my concern that there was already an excessive number of respiratory products on the list and that a detailed review of that list was necessary. He replaced two existing respirators on the list with the new respirator he selected. He determined that the new respirator, although slightly more expensive, could be used in the various applications where the existing respirators were used.

This is a good example of how it is important to work with employees that have the experience and authority needed to make effective item specification decisions. It is essential to assure that the appropriate personnel are involved when standardizing on items that can affect regulatory compliance and worker safety. Recognize that suppliers should only provide product information related to regulatory compliance and never claim that any given product can assure compliance with any given regulatory standard. Not only do they otherwise subject themselves to liability, it is the responsibility of personnel internal to your organization to make item selection decisions that assure compliance.

I advocate a simple New Item Requisition process that does not encumber the ability to get new items quickly:

1. Identify the reason the item is needed.

2. Confirm no existing item can support the need.

3. Review item and sourcing options.

4. Specify the item selected by documenting the manufacturer and manufacturer part number.

5. Procure the item selected.

Not much of a process, right? Consider, though, what must exist in an organization for this simple process to work.

1. There has to be known individuals that have been given the responsibility to select and source new items at the request of your employees.

2. There must be a method for employees to submit New Item Requisitions.

3. There has to be a known list of existing supply items in order for the requesting employee to confirm that a new supply item is needed.

4. The list of existing items must be current and readily available to all employees that may request a new item.

Now the simple New Item Requisition process could become much more complex to implement. In the next section, I talk about how to generate the Supply Item Master List; many organizations may have various supply item lists, but they are likely to be incomplete, relatively inaccessible, and limited to one or a few supply item categories.

At www.LeanTCO.com, we offer a simple on-line database solution that can be readily accessed by your employees. The database includes a New Item Requisition feature that allows your organization to track all employee requests for new supply items. You can immediately control the introduction of new supply items at the same time you begin building your master list.

It is important to assign responsibility to a limited number of employees for reviewing and approving New Item Requisitions; they will most likely be your employees with supply item purchasing authority. As you build your Supply Item Master List, it will become easier for the employees who have selection and sourcing responsibility to review any existing product alternatives and promote standardization.

Generate the Supply Item Master List

As a supplier, I had the opportunity to respond to a large, multi-facility quote request. The parent company was seeking to consolidate suppliers across twenty-plus facilities in the US and hired a large consulting firm to manage the quote process. We had to take the information we were provided and identify any missing manufacturer's part numbers in order to quote accurately. We often went in circles with the prospective customer and various manufacturers as we tried to identify the specific items that we should quote.

If your organization decides to obtain quotes for supply items, the use of manufacturer part numbers is essential not only to the ability of your current and prospective suppliers to quote efficiently, but for you to know exactly what you want quoted. Subtle differences in product descriptions can cause variance in what suppliers quote and can make analysis of quote responses extremely difficult. Take the example of hearing protection products. Earplugs are commonly offered in "corded" and "un-corded" versions where the corded version has the pair of earplugs connected by some form of a strand. Earplugs can also be individually packaged by the pair. It is common for one style of earplug to come in these various forms; if a quote request only specifies the manufacturer and style rather than a manufacturer's part number, vendors may quote the wrong item.

This is not a significant concern if you are just quoting earplugs, but if you have a comprehensive supply quote submitted to a number of potential suppliers, analyzing the quote responses is going to be a substantial challenge if manufacturer part numbers are not used.

Your Supply Item Master List will provide the foundation for controlling the selection, sourcing, and use of all supply items at your facility. The Supply Item Master List is the collective specification of all of your supply items. It is essential that the list contain manufacturer part numbers so that you have accurate supply information along with the ability to effectively control sourcing of those supplies.

I suggest that the following information be included on your Supply Item Master List:

1. Internal Item Number
2. Item Status
3. Item Category
4. Manufacturer Name
5. Manufacturer Part Number
6. Description
7. Purchase Unit of Measure (UOM)
8. Packaging
9. Source Code
10. Alternative Source
11. Replenishment Code

12. Reorder Point (in UOM)

13. Maximum Quantity on Hand (Max QOH)

14. Stocking Location

15. Consume First

16. Comments

The <u>Internal Item Number</u> is the number that will be used by your organization to track all information related to that item. I recommend the use of a simple, sequentially assigned number (i.e. 00001, 00002, 00003, ...) that does not have any coding significance; this allows your internal numbers to be generated without any effort or confusion. There are two primary reasons to use internal numbers: manufacturer part numbers can be complex and they can change. It is also easier to track alternative items when appropriate.

The <u>Item Status</u> indicates whether the item is Active, Inactive, Pending Disposition, or Under Evaluation. I recommend that you include items under evaluation on your list so that employees are aware of a potential new item. If you have a tool under evaluation that is not identified on the list, an employee may requisition another version of that tool rather than the version of the tool that is currently under consideration. I also recommend that you retain inactive items on your list. Supply items that have become inactive should not be re-introduced into your organization without review. The reason an item was inactivated can be included in the Comments section (see below). Items that are becoming inactive but are still in inventory are defined as Pending Disposition. (Visit www.LeanTCO.com to learn about using the online collaboration feature in our Supply Control Systems software to support item disposition.)

The <u>Item Category</u> is a category that you assign to each supply item. Examples of Item Categories would be janitorial products, fasteners, first aid supplies, and so on. Your Item Categories should be broad enough that you do not have small numbers of unique items in each category. An excessive number of categories can create unnecessary complexity in assigning items to those categories. We have already discussed <u>Manufacturer Name</u> and <u>Manufacturer Part Number</u> considerations at length. Remember *not* to use *supplier* part numbers.

Entering the <u>Description</u> of a supply item into the list will require some discipline. It is not necessarily sufficient to use the manufacturer's description since they vary in format, quality, and detail. When you create the description, if it is too simple or generic, it can be more difficult for employees to find and use the supply item based upon description information. I recommend sectionalizing the description of an item with commas, where each "section" of the description adds progressive detail to the definition of the item. The first word or phrase of the description should be generic and in ALL CAPS so that it stands out on a list of items. Common items should all use the same first word or phrase so that they are grouped together when they are sorted electronically by description.

The Purchase Unit of Measure (UOM) needs to be distinguished from the Issue Unit of Measure (IUOM) in order to assure proper tracking of inventory. Again using the example of earplugs, they are typically purchased by the box and issued by the pair. If the earplugs come 100 pairs to the box, an error in the Unit of Measure could lead to an inventory or purchasing error by a factor of 100. The Unit of Measure is not necessarily based upon the standard purchase quantity. If the earplugs are typically purchased 10 boxes to a case, it is still likely that "box" will be the UOM. The standard packaging, though, is critical information with respect to Total Cost of Ownership. The Packaging field is where you enter the standard packaging for the product. For the earplugs, that would look this:

100 pr/bx, 10 bx/cs

The case quantity is important if your organization uses a sufficient volume of the product to justify case purchases. It is much less expensive for your suppliers to ship in standard case quantities. Not only does it reduce supplier material handling costs, it also can reduce your freight costs depending upon how a partial case order would otherwise be shipped. Also, be certain to use consistent abbreviations for the Unit of Measure and Packaging fields. If you use "bx" for "box" and "cs" for "case", use those abbreviations consistently. Also, I recommend the format shown for all Packaging entries. Go from the smallest package to the largest package, separated by commas. If you purchase a product by the skid, the packaging entry might look like the following:

10/bx, 12 bx/cs, 24 cs/skid

I will digress for a moment to how your suppliers package your orders for shipment. As a supplier, we occasionally received orders from our sources in multiple small boxes rather than in single large boxes. For example, an order of 10 boxes of an item that weighs 3 pounds per box can be consolidated into a larger, single box if the individual boxes are small enough. If the individual boxes are 6" x 6" x 6", they can all be placed in a single 6" x 12" x 30" box. The shipping cost might be reduced by a factor of 5 in this scenario. When appropriate, we place requirements on our Purchase Orders for how product is to be packaged for shipment. With your own suppliers, I encourage you to audit how product is packaged for shipment to confirm that freight costs are being minimized... even if your supplier is "paying" the freight. As I discuss in detail later, all "free" supply chain costs are diverted back to the customer in the form of prices paid. More importantly, you should be working with your suppliers as strategic partners to minimize all partnership costs. More on that later as well.

The <u>Source Code</u> identifies the supplier for the item. I encourage the use of a single supplier, even if you have multiple sources where price competitiveness may change back and forth between the suppliers. The value of standardized sourcing will most likely outweigh occasional prices paid benefits. The <u>Alternative Source</u> field is where you identify a back-up source if the primary source cannot support an order.

The <u>Replenishment Code</u> is the method by which you determine the need to purchase the item. There are a variety of options depending upon how you choose to manage your inventory. If you use Visual Supply Management (see Chapter 3), cycle counts and kanban levels will be your primary methods of inventory control. You may also have some Vendor Managed Inventory (VMI). I recommend that you identify all individual supply items including those that are under VMI control. This allows your organization to have access to information on all supply items and also allows you to readily quote VMI items if the need should arise. The following are example Replenishment Codes:

Code	Description
VMI	Vendor Managed Inventory
CC3TUE	Cycle count on the 3rd Tuesday of the month
CCMON	Cycle count every Monday
CC24FRI	Cycle count on the 2nd and 4th Friday of the month
MINQOH	Purchased when the Reorder Point is reached

The <u>Reorder Point</u> is the QOH at which an order requirement is triggered. It is important to consider how Reorder Points will affect your order frequency. If all of your supply requirements are driven by Reorder Points, you could have an excessive number of low-dollar Purchase Orders occurring. If you use Reorder Points, be certain that the quantities you set are large enough that you can avoid immediately placing Purchase Orders. I recommend the use of cycle counts in combination with Reorder Points. Cycle counts are a means to gather order requirements across a large number of items simultaneously. Requirements triggered by Reorder Points can be combined with the results from the following scheduled cycle count, allowing fewer, larger volume Purchase Orders. More on this in the next chapter.

The <u>Maximum Quantity on Hand</u> (Max QOH) field is essential to maintaining proper inventory organization. Once space for an item has been allocated in a stocking area, exceeding that allocated space can create substantial inventory management challenges. If you are overstocked on an item and have inventory of that item in two locations as a result, your processes for pulling, counting, and reordering that item will be adversely affected.

The <u>Stocking Location</u> is the physically identified location for storage of the item. It is *not* all of the potential locations of the item, only the location where the item is stocked for distribution within your facility. For example, if you have supply cabinets in your facility where employees access inventory items, I recommend that you maintain a separate storage location for the item that can be used to replenish the cabinet locations and drive purchasing requirements. Your ordering activity is based upon the inventory in the single storage location, eliminating the need to count inventory in the multiple supply cabinets. In our Supply Control Systems online inventory management solution, we refer to your supply cabinets as Access Locations (visit www.LeanTCO.com for details).

The Consume First field is used to identify a useable alternative item that is becoming inactive on your Supply Item Master List. This supports the use of otherwise obsolete inventory and allows you to avoid purchasing inventory of the standard item until the alternative item is consumed.

The Comments field is used for any additional item details that you would like to record. Use the Comments field sparingly so that it does not become cluttered with relatively unimportant information.

The next section addresses inventory organization. If you have considerable work to do in this area, I recommend that the inventory organization effort be completed before the creation of the Supply Item Master List.

(We offer an online solution for managing your supply item inventory. The item information we just discussed is retained in a database that can be readily accessed by your employees. Security levels are used to control access to updating the information in the database. New Item Requisitions can be submitted by any user and the corresponding item selection and sourcing activity can be effectively managed. This online solution supports automated, simultaneous generation of Purchase Requisitions across all of your supply items and source codes. In addition, key supply-related decisions can be communicated and documented through online collaboration. Visit www.LeanTCO.com for details.)

Apply 5S Principles and Get Organized

If comprehensive item specification is the foundation of our TCO reduction effort, the application of 5S principles is the grading of the land and the installation of the concrete forms that occurs before that foundation is poured. We will begin with a quick overview of 5S and then provide the detailed steps to follow as you get your inventory fully organized and into known stocking locations.

5S is a methodology for workplace organization that is intended to improve efficiency, safety, and morale. The ability to readily obtain a needed item is one of the key efficiency concepts behind 5S. If an item is always placed in a known location, no time is lost searching for that item. Each S in 5S methodology represents a Japanese word that begins with the letter S when translated to English. The following are abbreviated and paraphrased definitions for each word:

> **Sorting:** Keeping only essential items. Everything else is stored or discarded.
>
> **Straighten (Set in Order):** Arranging items to promote efficiency, setting items in an order that supports efficient flow.
>
> **Sweeping (Shining):** Regular cleaning that maintains the organization and cleanliness of a work area.
>
> **Standardizing:** Implementing consistent and standard work practices.

Sustaining: Assuring that gains are retained and that further improvements are supported.

Our primary objective in the application of 5S to supply inventory is to accomplish the following:

"A place for everything
and everything in its place."

It sounds simplistic, but if you walk into the typical supply stockroom, the thought of getting everything you see into known inventory locations can be overwhelming. The following steps can make the task much easier:

1. Install a sufficient amount of flexible shelving to get the inventory organized. Do not use cabinets unless absolutely necessary; they limit Visual Supply Management (see the next chapter) and are easier to use as hidden storage locations for unauthorized items.

2. Arrange the shelving in a manner that inventory locations can be easily identified (for example, C-2-3 could represent shelving row C, shelving unit 2, shelf number 3). Work with your Safety Department to assure that any safety-related storage requirements are satisfied (i.e. flammable cabinets).

3. Get all inventory into locations, grouping items by item category. Do not document the items or attempt to identify inactive items, just get the inventory organized. Recognize that additional space may need to be allocated for some items after the Maximum Quantity on Hand numbers are determined. Assure that there is only one

item in each location; do not "hide" items behind other items of a different type.

4. Identify each item and enter the item information into the Supply Item Master List, including location information. Print labels for each item on the list, including the Item Number, Manufacturer, Manufacturer Number, Item Category, Description, Reorder Point, Maximum QOH, and Location. Visit www.LeanTCO.com to learn about how you can manage inventory locations and labeling with our online inventory control solution.

5. When reviewing each item, confirm with the appropriate personnel that the item should have an "Active" status. For all other items, determine if the item is usable and can be consumed. If so, identify any corresponding Active item that should not be used ahead of the discontinued item. Enter the discontinued item as a Consume First item in the Active item record.

6. For Inactive items, identify disposition in the Comments field. Common entries would include review, consume, discard, and return to vendor.

The process of identifying inactive items should include documentation of the reason those items have been made inactive. This information can be placed in the Comments field and can help reduce the risk of the item being purchased again in the future. (Visit www.LeanTCO.com to learn about our Supply Control Systems software feature for documenting supply item decisions through online collaboration.)

One last thought regarding 5S. When your Lean TCO Program team is reviewing and improving supply related processes, apply 5S principles to the corresponding work areas. For processes to be efficient, employees need to have work areas that support smooth work flow, have a place for everything, and have everything in its place.

Chapter 3

Visual Supply Management

Visual Supply Management techniques can be used as an efficient and effective alternative to more traditional transaction-based inventory control systems. Dependable inventory restocking methods are essential to minimizing TCO. You may need to implement new methods to identify when supply items need to be reordered, or you may simply need to improve your existing methods. I strongly recommend that you give serious consideration to the use of Visual Supply Management.

The Expense of Transaction-Based Control

Organizations can erroneously jump to the conclusion that effective inventory control requires inventory transactions for all material movement. Some organizations implement expensive solutions to support those transactions; a 10 cent supply item can carry with it 90 cents in transaction costs if these solutions are not implemented carefully.

A large customer of my supply business used inventory transactions to manage supply items. They, like many organizations, made a substantial investment in software and training to control their supply inventory. We received software-generated Purchase Orders from their automated system. The average order size was extremely small compared to our other accounts since their system was triggering Purchase Orders whenever any item of those we supplied hit a minimum stocking level. Not only were their freight costs extremely high as a percentage of prices paid, so were our internal costs in supporting that transaction-based system.

This type of inventory control was still better than others we experienced. We received an urgent call from a local account. The buyer was out of a few items that he desperately needed and he asked if we could ship those items that day. We did. A few days later he called again, in need of the same items we had shipped a few days prior. We explained that his usage rate on those items was too low for him to already have stock outs, but he urged us to make an immediate same-day delivery. We did. Not only did we place the items in our rush delivery onto his shelves, we did the same with the items that were shipped a few days prior. Unknown to him, the rush shipment was sitting on the floor in the stockroom. The urgent shipment and the rush delivery added up to less than $500 in product. Consider for a moment all of the costs incurred by our customer and my company in getting that $500 in product available to end-users. Also consider the fact that the stock outs on those items spanned 3 days.

If an organization is experiencing that level of difficulty in controlling supply items, it is understandable that management may jump into expensive inventory control solutions. It is also understandable that they may jump into a Vendor Managed Inventory solution without sufficient analysis based upon a well-timed sales presentation from a supplier.

When we would hear the phrase "I am completely out of..." from one of our customers, we were not looking forward to processing the corresponding order. We were bracing ourselves for what would become a very expensive business transaction. This was an important experience when it came to the development of Lean TCO; as a supplier that would occasionally *fear* customer orders, I gave that fear a great deal of thought. Not all customer orders are good orders, and my organization either had to revert the corresponding losses of those orders back on our customer base in order to maintain profitability targets, or we simply had to absorb those losses. Neither alternative seemed "fair" with respect to business ethics or business finances. My attention turned to the cause of the rush low-dollar orders that were so expensive to my company and how my customers might gain better control of their inventory. I quickly realized that most of my customers could not justify the cost of transactions to manage their inventory; it was during those early days that the important building blocks of Lean TCO were being formed.

Organizations that pursue transaction based inventory control often look to reduce the cost of those transactions through the implementation of barcodes. One of my business experiences was as a distributor of music CD's. The business was responsible for receiving, managing, labeling, and distributing the CD inventory. On average, over 10,000 CD's made their way through our warehouse each day, destined for over 1000 potential retail locations that would receive CD's from us at least once per month. I mention this because that business eventually applied over 5 million barcodes to products... so many barcodes that I eventually utilized my engineering background and lean expertise to develop a large collating machine for processing the CD's. So when it comes to barcodes, I have some experience.

I am not going to make a blanket statement that barcodes should not be used, but the cost of applying barcodes in order to automate inventory transactions requires close analysis if it is going to be considered by your organization. Manually applying a label to a product is surprisingly expensive, and you need to think in terms of dimes, not pennies, to get one label affixed to one supply item. Before pursuing a barcode solution, conduct time studies that include all of the material handling necessary to support applying labels.

The benefit of a supply item with a barcode is clear. If your supply control solution includes inventory transactions when supplies are given to employees, a scan of a barcode is much faster than manual data entry. Barcodes also eliminate the risk of data entry errors. Remember, though, that all transactions induce cost and they may not be needed at all. We explore that idea in the next section.

The Power of Visual Control

As the head of Engineering for a division of a large corporation, I hired a New Product Development Manager that had considerable experience with project management software. We began to implement the software product that he was most familiar with, the leading project management software at the time, for all of our new product development activity. It wasn't long before I noticed that my New Product Development Manager was spending most of his time at his desk analyzing and updating project schedules. Maintaining accurate schedules was certainly important, but his real value to my Engineering team was in his leadership skills rather than his project management software skills.

Project scheduling software has a powerful feature that allows you to tie the end of one task to the beginning of another. This is called *dependency*, where you can't start a dependant task until the corresponding prior task has been completed. Once task dependencies are established in the project schedule, task start dates, end dates, and durations can be changed and all of the tasks in the project will shift along the project timeline accordingly. The dependencies also create was is called the "critical path", the series of dependent tasks that produce the overall amount of time that will be required to complete the project.

If a project schedule was unacceptably long in my view, or would not meet the requirements of the Sales and Marketing department, I would study the project schedule and focus on task dependencies along the critical path. Elimination of task dependencies allows more tasks to be completed in parallel and reduces the overall length of the project. Injection molded parts use a mold that is placed into an injection press. These molds can be complex depending upon the size and design of the part as well as the number of parts the mold produces at one time. Conventional thinking was that you had to have completed the design of the plastic part before you could start the process of getting the mold designed and fabricated, and my Engineering staff was following that convention. When we defined that dependency in our project management software, the software simply reinforced that we had to complete part design before we could procure the mold for the part.

In reality, I determined that if we had progressed to a point in the product design process where we knew the overall size of a plastic part, the number of parts the mold would need to produce at one time, and what features the mold would require in order to produce the parts, we could place the task of procuring the mold base... the basic components of the mold prior to machining for the detailed part design... in parallel with the final design phase of the part. Since procuring the mold base required several weeks, we were able to take several weeks out of each project schedule and substantially reduce our time-to-market for new products. We could accomplish these types of time savings by stepping back from the limitations of task dependencies defined in the project management software.

So how does this relate to inventory control of supply items? Consider a minimum stocking level. When inventory hits that level, it is time to restock. Let's say it is early April and your organization purchases winter-lined gloves for work activity performed during the winter months. Your inventory control system indicates that you have hit your minimum stocking level for the gloves. Do you bring in more of the gloves? How many pairs? Consider a situation where a given item hits a minimum stocking level and an alternative item is currently being evaluated as a potential replacement. Do you bring in more of that item? Do you have time to wait for the evaluation of the alternative item? What if you carry an inventory of rain suits. What has the weather been like? How much work is being performed outdoors? Are there any projects coming that will increase the amount of outdoor work?

We could come up with hundreds of examples where the human mind can process certain information about supply inventory far more effectively than even the most intelligently programmed inventory control software packages. There is financial risk when an organization turns control over to a system that will blindly generate supply item requirements. That does not mean software and/or minimum stocking levels should not be used... it simply means that the ideal inventory control solution will not rigidly generate requirements without appropriate human interaction.

That is where Visual Supply Management comes in. Visual Supply Management is a cost-effective alternative to transaction based inventory control solutions. The solution starts with all supply inventory in known, labeled stock locations. The inventory labels describe the product in the location and also contain suggested minimum and maximum stocking levels. Those responsible for maintaining on-hand inventory perform a scheduled visual check of inventory levels.

The timing of the inventory checks can be determined in a number of ways. For example, if your organization plans to maintain a minimum on-hand inventory that represents 2 weeks of usage, inventory checks could occur every two weeks. Those checks could be performed across all items at one time, or they could be spread out over a number of days according to groups of items. More critical items could be counted more frequently.

Early in the launch of my supply business, I provided this type of service on-site for one of our customers. I was the primary supplier of consumable supply items and the inventory of those items was maintained in one room. I organized the inventory and labeled each inventory location. I made one monthly visit, bringing the inventory that I determined was needed from the prior visit and placing it into stock. Approximately 150 items were involved. This was a form of Vendor Managed Inventory that worked quite well.

The use of Visual Supply Management was so effective that I could reasonably predict what I would need to bring for the *next* monthly visit from a visual review of current inventory. Within a few months, I developed a strong visual sense of how the inventory moved. I could glance at an inventory location and know immediately whether or not I should bring more of that item for the next visit, *even though that next visit would not occur for another four weeks.* I also developed a good visual sense of how much room there was for each item... I rarely brought more of an item than would fit in the allocated space. I also knew which items were seasonal and could adjust order quantities accordingly. The ability to use Visual Supply Management to project inventory needs that would exist 4 weeks later is a strong argument for how well it can work for identifying current inventory needs.

I should comment on my views of this Vendor Managed Inventory service I was providing. It was effective and it served the customer well. It was an important learning experience. *It was also extremely expensive.* On average, it would take me about 30 minutes to re-organize misplaced inventory, put my delivered items into their proper locations, and dispose of packaging. It would then take me about 10 minutes to perform the visual check of the 150 or so supply items and record order quantities for the next visit. I was in and out in less than one hour. This customer was about 45 minutes from our warehouse, so there was 90 minutes of drive time to perform 40 minutes of work. There were also vehicle operating expenses involved. I eventually encouraged the customer to perform the same visual checks, produce their own orders, and stock their own shelves. We were able to reduce our prices while maintaining the same level of profit, so it was better for us *as well as the customer* to move the VMI service activities in-house.

Here are some key considerations when implementing Visual Supply Management:

1. As covered in the previous chapter, assure all inventory is in properly labeled locations. The labels must include the Reorder Point and the Maximum Quantity on Hand.

2. Establish a cycle count schedule based upon inventory minimums and projected usage rates.

3. When performing the inventory check, go shelf-to-shelf in a continuous pattern. *Do not* skip inventory locations.

4. Use a form printed in Item Number order to record order quantities. *Do not* look at an item on the form and then try to find that item on the shelf.

5. Be certain your printed form has standard packaging information so that items can be ordered in package quantities when appropriate.

6. When inventory arrives, make certain that all existing inventory is in proper locations and then place the ordered items onto the shelving. Use First-In-First-Out (FIFO), placing new inventory behind existing inventory on the shelving.

This method can be applied to any number of supply items across any number of commodity categories. I recommend a copy of the VSM form be kept in each supply area so that employees can note on the form if the inventory level of an item is getting low. This will not only assure that the item gets ordered but can also eliminate unproductive emails and phone calls to the Purchasing Department. Visit www.LeanTCO.com to learn about our on-line solution for Visual Supply Management.

Visual Supply Management and Kanban

I was running an Engineering team for a contract electronics manufacturer at a time when a new account was producing some significant challenges for my employer. The ownership of the company knew that I had a lean background and asked if I would step in and help with an off-site production facility that could not achieve target production levels. I declined.

So much of what lean experts need to do in order to achieve dramatic improvements goes against conventional wisdom. In this situation, decisions were being made by my peers... the other department heads in the company... that were logical at that time. I knew that if I were to step in and provide guidance from a lean perspective, there would be tremendous resistance from my peers; these were people that I respected and enjoyed working with and I did not have the authority to impact their areas of responsibility.

The circumstances with the new account were complicated by the fact that the customer had designed the product we were building on their behalf. There were design flaws that needed to be corrected, and the manufacturing team was unable to overcome those design flaws and meet production requirements. As is common with batch manufacturing approaches, subassemblies were being built in substantial volumes. Many of the subassemblies were not passing quality inspections and/or functional tests. As raw components were being consumed at increasing rates to try and get a sufficient number of subassemblies through inspection and testing, raw component purchases were skyrocketing. Production quotas were increasing to try and cover previous production shortfalls.

The new account became increasingly important to my employer as substantial losses needed to be recovered. As the customer was threatening to pull the contract, the Sales Department was insistent on being supportive and responsive to the customer at all cost. The customer wanted to know that targeted production volumes would be increasing as the need for their product in the marketplace grew.

The owners approached me a second time, and I again declined. I explained that the methods I would need to employ would not only frustrate and confuse my peers but the owners themselves. I expressed that there was no time for team building and training to build support for lean methodology and suggested that they stop the losses and let the account go. This was not what they wanted to hear from their head of Engineering.

It was not reasonable for me to expect that a highly successful and rapidly growing contract manufacturer would accept my new ideas without preparation. They were, and continue to be, a highly successful company. I am a team player and I knew that there would have been no opportunity to build a team consensus fast enough to save the account.

83 employees were dedicated to building this product at an offsite facility. They were attempting to build 500 units per day and sufficient raw material was being brought in to support that target volume. The group was yielding fewer than 200 units per day and nonconforming subassemblies filled their production area.

The third time the owners approached me I described the only circumstances under which there might be some hope to salvage the account. I explained that every department, from Sales to Quality, would not be supportive of what I knew needed to be done. I explained that they, the owners, would also be upset at the decisions I would be making, and that those decisions would be occurring at a rapid-fire pace.

The owners of the business agreed to "turn the keys over to me" on this account and I went to work. I respected the fact that they were able to make such a difficult and unconventional decision. It was, though, difficult for them to accept the first few days of the changes I implemented.

My first action was to return 30 of the 83 employees back to the main facility. My employer had been staffing up the offsite facility as quickly as they could and did not want to see all of the work and expense in obtaining that manufacturing staff go to waste. Those employees were re-deployed in other manufacturing activity, which made my first difficult decision much easier. My second action was to stop all purchasing activity for the product until further notice.

Everyone knew how far behind we were and how important it had been to keep raw material flowing into the company, so this decision was also met with considerable skepticism. It is not easy to get the procurement wheels turning again after they are brought to a complete stop, but I was unwilling to purchase any component until I knew it was going to be usable. There was no time to analyze each component so the entire procurement machine had to be shut down.

My third action was to remove all discrepant subassemblies from the production area and redeploy a number of production workers to assist technicians in repairing the subassemblies or breaking them back down into individual components. We began scrapping anything unusable.

My fourth action was to reduce the daily production target from 500 units to 1. I spoke to the remaining production line workers and suggested that they bring a good book if they liked to read. I indicated that if we had a successful day building 1 unit we would try 5 the following day, but I was not making any commitments until I confirmed we could build 1 without creating any scrap.

I had the Sales Department inform our customer that their product was not production-ready due to some design flaws, but that our Engineering Department would work with them to correct those flaws. This all occurred in the first two days. You can imagine the talk around the office. "There goes the account. Not only has he stopped procurement and shut down production, he has people tearing down assemblies and throwing parts away. On top of that, he is insulting the customer by telling them their product design is flawed."

It was admittedly ugly. There was nothing pretty about making such harsh assessments and taking corresponding actions. I had know idea if we were going to succeed, I just knew that these early steps were essential if we were to have a chance.

With engineers and technicians at the offsite facility, we cleared the production area of all Work-In-Progress (WIP) and built one unit. We documented some of the design and production issues and began corrective action work. The following day we built 5. We moved more people from the offsite facility back to the main facility. We took more corrective action to fix other design and process flaws we were uncovering. As we re-established the production line, we only allowed the raw material needed to build that day's target production volume to move from the stocking area into the production area. If at any step in the process there was any problem, the entire line stopped until the problem was corrected.

We implemented every aspect of a controlled, pull-driven manufacturing system. Worker A was not able to perform an assembly task until downstream worker B had taken the unit worker A had just completed. If worker J had an unresolved problem, workers A through I were sitting idle with their single completed units waiting on the right side of their workstations. The Production Supervisor would know immediately if there was a problem anywhere in the process because the entire production line would quickly come to a stop.

If there was a component problem, design problem, process problem, or worker error that caused the stoppage, it was easy to work our way upstream through the process and find out what had changed. Sometimes the line was stopped only for a few moments as corrective action was implemented immediately, other times the production line was stopped for hours as we descended on a major corrective action effort.

As we became more confident in our ability to produce the product successfully, we would increase our production plan for the following day. As our efficiency gains exceeded our planned production volumes, we moved more workers from the offsite facility to the main facility. It eventually became necessary to restart the procurement machine in preparation for full-run production.

As production volumes were increasing, it became more important that individual workers remained productive. When a worker cannot complete an assembly task until the worker to their right has taken the WIP just completed, any short-term imbalance in the production line can result in lost productivity. Since we were no longer building scrap, we could allow each worker to build slightly ahead of the downstream need. Depending upon the assembly task, perhaps we would allow the worker to have up to 5 completed units to their right before they had to stop. In that way, if one worker in the process produced a short-term imbalance, the overall production line continued and the momentary imbalance appropriately went unnoticed.

Within approximately 16 weeks, we achieved our daily production target of 500 units with a production staff of 26 employees, representing an eight-fold increase in productivity. This was accomplished through the rigorous implementation of unbreakable rules, rules that on the surface appeared counter-productive, but rules that resulted in more than an 80% reduction in labor cost per unit.

Your Lean TCO Program team should learn from this story not only about kanban levels, which we will discuss shortly, but from the benefits of employing any disciplined methodology. The degree of success your Lean TCO Program team experiences will be directly proportional to the degree of success they have in implementing healthy supply-related disciplines. I hope your team will have an experience similar to the one I just shared. The success of that lean manufacturing effort came from the hard work of a large number of people. Not every idea that was implemented in that effort was my own, and tremendous progress was made by that group when I was off running the Engineering Department. I was not there for every decision or every corrective action, I was simply the bad guy that needed to implement the unbreakable rules:

> We don't purchase potential scrap.
> We don't assemble potential scrap.

We operate balanced production lines.

We go directly to the source of problems (even if the customer is that source).

And so on.

Your team will facilitate the creation and implementation of the rules, but the overall success of your Lean TCO Program will be to the credit of the team *and* all of your employees that adopt and embrace those rules.

I would also like your team to see the power of *visual control* in this story. How was the Production Supervisor notified of a production problem? Visually. There was no email, computer report, or production meeting that revealed the production issue. It was a visual recognition that production activity had gone idle. How quickly was the Production Supervisor made aware of the production problem? Immediately. At a glance, the supervisor knew to take action.

Back to kanban. Kanban is a Japanese word that has been associated with lean and Just-In-Time (JIT) methodologies. Specifically, *kan* means "visual" and *ban* means "board." In lean applications, the term kanban is commonly used to refer to something visual that triggers an action. In the production process improvement effort, the visual trigger for production workers in the assembly line was a kanban level. If the kanban level was set to 5, the worker was not to complete their assembly task until their were 4 or fewer completed units on the right side of their workstation. To say it another way, when the kanban level of 5 units was reached, the worker was triggered to stop.

Organizations are successfully applying kanban to the control supply inventory. There are two commonly used methods.

The first method applies the use of cards that contain the supply item information and the reorder point for the item. Depending upon the packaging and storage method of the supply item, the kanban card can be inserted into the inventory of the item such that it is revealed when the reorder point is reached. When the card is revealed, it is time to restock. If the supply item is a roll of tape, for example, the card can be inserted at the appropriate point between the rolls. The rolls behind the card represent the reorder point. When the roll of tape immediately in front of the card is taken, the card is revealed and placed in a known location (such as a specified bin on a desk) so that the tape is ordered.

A similar kanban approach uses two inventory bins for each item rather than cards. Both bins are labeled with the item information. In the storage location, one bin is placed in front of the other bin. The rear bin contains enough inventory of the item to last until that item is restocked... it contains the reorder point quantity. When the front bin is emptied, it is placed in a known location so that the item is ordered.

Using kanban cards or bins can be an effective alternative for items that cannot be readily ordered by a visual scan alone. Examples would include the following:

- Items that have irregular usage patterns

- Items that have unknown usage patterns

- Stocking areas with a very large number of unique items

The use of kanban techniques requires minimal training and offers a secure method of controlling inventory if the discipline of proper card and/or bin usage is retained. (One customer told me a story of her own attempt to implement kanban cards... she said it would have worked fine if employees had not thrown the cards on the floor when reorder points were reached!)

The primary limitation of this approach is that it can be difficult to manage fluctuating inventory requirements. Once dependence is created on kanban cards or bins to reorder supply items, there is the risk that items that are not needed will be ordered (i.e. winter-lined work gloves ordered in May). There is also the risk that an increasing need for an item will not be recognized if the corresponding reorder point is not adjusted.

When implementing a kanban solution, be aware that the triggers to order inventory can occur continuously. Kanban cards or bins can be indicating the need to purchase inventory at any time. Consider a situation where on Monday a kanban card triggers the purchase of an item from Supplier A. If that item is purchased immediately, and there is no other need for any other items from Supplier A, there is risk that your overhead costs for that purchase will be considerable. If then on Tuesday another kanban card for Supplier A triggers another purchase, the opportunity to consolidate those orders is gone. If this is occurring in a large organization with a large number of suppliers, Purchase Orders could be fired off in a frenzy and result in substantially increased Total Cost of Ownership. I mentioned earlier that I have this same concern for transaction-based inventory control systems.

This risk can be mitigated by *scheduled* visual scans of inventory and *scheduled* Purchase Order placements with suppliers. Rather than simply waiting for a kanban card to be revealed or a for a kanban bin to be emptied, a scheduled inventory scan can capture requirements already triggered by kanban techniques *as well as* any inventory that is approaching the reorder quantity.

If this approach is followed, the reorder quantities must be large enough to span the supplier lead time for the item as well as the time between scheduled Purchase Orders for the supplier. If the scheduled PO frequency for the supplier is once every 2 weeks, supplier lead time for the item is 1 week, and an additional 2 weeks of safety stock is applied, the reorder point for the item would be equal to 5 weeks of item usage.

In the above example, what would be a reasonable order quantity for the item? There are four considerations:

- minimum order frequency
- standard item packaging
- available shelf space
- the cost of the item

The item can be ordered as frequently as once every 2 weeks, so no less than 2 weeks of item consumption should be ordered at one time. That does not mean that 2 weeks of consumption produces the right order quantity. Again using the example of work gloves, they are often purchased by the dozen and issued by the pair. If your expected rate of consumption is 20 pairs per week, you would not order 20 pairs. You might consider ordering 24 pairs. What if the work gloves are sold 5 dozen to the case? Remember your supplier partnership objective to reduce all mutual costs, not just internal costs. It is much less expensive per pair for the supplier to ship a full case of gloves as opposed to a partial case of gloves.

Before ordering the full case of gloves, you need to consider the amount of shelf space allocated for the gloves. Well controlled inventory can quickly become out of control if the quantities of items purchased exceed allocated space. The excess inventory would need to be placed somewhere, and the next time a reorder point is hit for that item, it would be necessary to find that excess inventory if an unneeded purchase is to be avoided.

Finally, it might be important to consider the cost of the item. If the work gloves were lined in gold and cost $250.00 per pair, you would probably want to limit the purchase to 24 pair. Conversely, if the gloves were $0.01 per pair, you do not want to be placing frequent orders and you might consider filling the allocated space for the item with each purchase. In general, though, the cost of an item should not influence the size of the purchase. The carrying cost for supply inventory is usually inconsequentially low... unlike raw material inventory for manufacturing organizations... so it is rarely necessary to consider the expense of an item as a driver for purchase quantity decisions.

In summary, the use of Visual Supply Management is a cost effective alternative to transaction based inventory control. Kanban cards or bins can be used to supplement visual inventory scans where necessary. As with any process improvement, disciplines must be applied to assure that all process steps are properly followed in order to maximize the benefit of the improvement effort.

Automate Purchase Requisitions

You have seen my shameless promotional references to www.LeanTCO.com throughout this book. This section on automating supply item requisitions relates to a particular feature of our online supply control software. As you complete the process of getting your inventory organized and creating your Supply Item Master List, a natural automation opportunity results. If you are using Source Codes to identify the supplier for each item on your list, and if you are using Visual Supply Management, you have a method of controlling your supply inventory that becomes independent of supply item categories and supply item sources. With all of your supply items under one method of control, you are simultaneously generating purchasing requirements for supply items that may come from multiple suppliers.

If you are using our online Supply Control Systems software, you can enter the item quantity requirements from your Visual Supply Management forms (that can also be printed from the software) and generate Purchase Requisitions at one time across all affected suppliers. By generating automated Purchase Requisitions rather than automated Purchase Orders, you are able to use the requisitions to create orders within whatever software your organization currently uses for procurement (such as an ERP system). Our online software can simply serve as a front-end to your standard procurement methods.

The software allows you to generate and print individual Purchase Requisitions by Source Code from any given Visual Supply Management entry of item order quantities. You can also copy these requisitions into a spreadsheet format so that they can be transferred electronically into your procurement system if appropriate. Whether your Visual Supply Management entries span 25 or 2500 items, and whether they span 2 or 20 suppliers, the software will break down the item requirements by supplier in order to facilitate rapid Purchase Order generation. This is not only significant from a lean Total Cost of Ownership perspective, it is significant from a lead time perspective. The faster you are able to convert inventory requirements into Purchase Orders, the faster you will have that inventory replenished and available to your employees. An additional benefit of quick replenishment is the increased potential to consolidate orders. For example, if a kanban card is pulled in order for the corresponding item to be purchased, shorter inventory replenishment times will increase the amount of time that the card can "sit" as it awaits the next Visual Supply Management inventory scan.

Chapter 4

Know Your Supply Procurement Options

The complexity of supply item procurement, which some argue is far greater than the complexity of raw material procurement, is defined by the myriad of options that buyers face when selecting and sourcing a supply item. Your Lean TCO Program team will need to be aware of these options and develop a sense of the challenges that lie ahead. We start this chapter with a look at a seemingly insignificant commodity item that is used in all organizations.

<u>Simple Commodities, Complex Alternatives</u>

Consider restroom soap dispensers. We all know what it is like to hit that little lever and experience disappointment when nothing comes out. We lean across to the other dispenser and experience the same result.... and if we are in a restaurant restroom at the time... the thought of the people preparing our food comes to mind. If we are at work, we might be a little annoyed with those responsible for what seems like such a simple task... making sure a soap dispenser will actually dispense soap.

One of the outcomes of your Lean TCO Program will be the transparency of your success. To those who look at the numbers, your success will be as visible as the shining sun. To those who *only use* supply items, you want such ease of supply item access and such dependable availability that they give those items as much thought as you give to soap in a restroom. We instinctively hit the soap dispenser lever without thinking... we only give thought to the soap when it isn't there. I am a fortunate man who has been married for 27 years at the time of writing this book. My wife is a very patient woman who deserves the credit for sticking with a man that admittedly takes too much for granted. If you're like me, you've heard it. "Do you think those clothes make it to washing machine and back into your dresser, neatly folded, all by themselves?" She's right, I never think about it. When I open the drawer, the clothing I need is there.

If you are reading this book as a buyer of consumables, I doubt you have ever gone home with worries about soap on your mind. I wouldn't be surprised, though, if you experience regular frustration with the challenge of keeping hundreds of supply items continuously available to those who need them. If you are not a buyer of consumables, respect the fact that these buyers are facing complex challenges across a broad array of supplies simultaneously, working to avoid everything from minor employee frustrations to the inability of employees to perform their job because a critical item is not available. Many buyers of consumable supplies feel that they have a thankless job and only get noticed when there are problems related to the items they purchase.

Back to the soap. We will consider a situation where a buyer has been given the "simple" task of sourcing hand soap for use in restrooms. I have not researched soap manufacturers and soap distribution channels specifically, so I will just throw out some numbers for the sake of our simple example. Let's say that there are 30 manufacturers of liquid soap used in commercial applications, that each manufacturer has an average of 10 different liquid soap alternatives (scents, lotion additives, anti-bacterial additives, foaming, and so on), and that each liquid soap alternative is available in an average of 4 different dispensing packages. That would be 1200 possible soap choices. All of these choices would be available to the buyer at a variety of prices and through a variety of distribution channels.

Let's further say that the buyer's organization does not currently have an outside janitorial service, but there has been some talk that outsourcing janitorial services might be a good idea. If an outside janitorial service checks the dispensers and adds soap as necessary, the soap becomes Vendor Managed Inventory (VMI). Now the buyer needs to consider integrating the possible sourcing of janitorial services into the already surprisingly complex soap decision.

What types of dispensers already exist in the restrooms? Are they all the same? If a janitorial service is brought into the mix, do they carry the type of soap that will work in the dispensers already in place? How much would it cost to replace the dispensers if that becomes necessary? If we refill the dispensers ourselves, who will do it and how will they know when to do it?

All of these thoughts might run through the typical buyer's mind in less than 30 seconds. If it is a less disciplined buyer, or if the buyer is simply overworked, they might reach for the phone and call the Maintenance Department, tell them to find out which dispenser is the most common in the restrooms and change out all of the others to be the same, and pick a soap out of a supplier's catalog. After all, it's just soap and it doesn't cost very much. Better yet, less than an hour after the buyer's supervisor brought up the soap issue, the buyer responds with a quick email saying it is already being taken care of.

Expand this example to all consumable supply decisions. It's just a pair of work gloves. It's just a broom. It's just a can of spray paint.

97

Quick, simple, and apparently efficient decisions being made throughout the organization, sometimes multiple times over for the same items, and suddenly the organization has $1,000,000 in annual supply-related indirect spend with another $500,000 in overhead costs. The breadth of alternatives for virtually any supply item is truly overwhelming, and if the organization does not have a framework for making the best selection and sourcing decision for each discrete item, what might have been a TCO of $750,000 has reached $1,500,000 and keeps growing.

Vendor On-Site Services

Vendor on-site services can add significant value, but they can also add significant cost. I have provided a variety of on-site services for my customers as a supply item distributor. Although I appreciated the business, I often felt I was doing work that could be performed by internal personnel at a much lower expense to the customer. When I was inspecting safety equipment according to the requirements of the Occupational Safety and Health Administration (OSHA), my customers were able to know that the work was being performed both dependably and accurately. If an OSHA auditor learned that those inspections were not performed as required, my customer could have received a substantial fine. More importantly, if an employee needed to use the safety equipment and that equipment was not functional, personal injury could have resulted. It was a logical decision on the part of my customer to use my services and expertise in that area. From a TCO perspective, though, was it the right decision?

This is a challenging example of vendor services to consider. First of all, if the internal knowledge for the equipment inspections did not exist and an outside service was not used, employee safety was at risk. The same would be true if internal knowledge did exist but issues surrounding employee workload or dependability resulted in equipment inspections being missed. In the overall scope of operating expenses, the percentage of spend on these equipment inspections was extremely small. Furthermore, any OSHA fines could have easily exceeded the annual expense for the service.

We will jump ahead for a moment and assume your Lean TCO Program team has the issue of equipment inspections under analysis. The team would first acknowledge that employee safety is the top priority. No risks to employee safety would result from a TCO reduction effort. With that as a given, what steps should be taken by the team? They would first talk to the employee responsible for safety; we will use the title "Safety Coordinator" in this example. They would ask the Safety Coordinator how the decision was made to outsource the inspection activity. There could have been a variety of reasons:

> "Our safety products supplier is in here every month to restock our safety inventory and he checks our equipment while he is here."

> "The equipment is complex and we don't have the expertise to perform the inspections."

> "We were hit with an OSHA fine two years ago for inspections not being done. We brought the supplier in to perform the inspections back then."

> "We don't have the time to perform the inspections ourselves."

> "We had trained someone in the Maintenance Department to do the inspections but they would never get them done on time."

We will break down the example responses as follows:

1. A supplier providing VMI services is already on-site.

2. Internal personnel are not trained to do inspections.

3. A fine occurred due to regulatory non-compliance.

4. There is a lack of manpower.

5. There is a lack of employee dependability.

The challenge to the Lean TCO Program team is to determine a course of action that is consistent with the overall objectives of the program. If the vendor is already on-site, is it likely that they will still be a vendor at the completion of the Lean TCO Program? Are the VMI services they provide consistent with minimized TCO? Is use of the outside service necessary to assure employee safety and avoid potential regulatory fines? Should the on-site service impact the vendor selection process? Can concerns surrounding manpower, training, and employee dependability be resolved? How is the vendor's product pricing impacted by the services provided?

These are complex questions that can only be answered with some effort by the program team and the Safety Coordinator. There are many interrelated factors that add to the complexity of obtaining those answers. The point, though, is simple. The team needs to fully understand the organization's current practices, why those practices are in place, and the full impact of changing those practices.

The TCO Program Team will need to look at all forms of vendor on-site services. A few examples include Vendor Managed Inventory (discussed in detail in Chapter 4), janitorial services, vending services, uniform services, equipment services, and inspection services. Those services that can ultimately be performed by internal personnel should be analyzed for potential TCO benefit. Remember that you are paying for the expense of service providers traveling to your facility even if there is no separate line item on an invoice (see Chapter 5).

Vendor Managed Inventory

Vendor Managed Inventory (VMI) can be a viable solution for many customer-supplier partnerships. I discuss in Chapter 5 my concern with the use of term "free freight", and for the same reasons outlined in that chapter, I also have concern with the use of the term "free" when it comes to VMI.

Consider the new car purchase as an analogy. You want to replace your current ride, and you walk into the dealership to check out a car that has caught your eye. A salesman approaches and at some point in the conversation asks you the same two questions that virtually every car salesman asks virtually every prospective buyer:

"How much of a monthly payment can you afford?"

and:

"Do you have a trade-in?"

If these questions are asked almost universally, there must be a very good reason as to why. That reason is simple: key tools in the control of the transaction are transferred from the buyer to the seller.

There is a fair price for the new car, and not a dollar more should be paid for it. There is a fair price for the trade-in, and not a dollar less should be taken for it. The job of the new car buyer is to achieve both. The job of the salesman is to maximize the price for the new car and minimize the price for the trade-in... in other words... to prevent the new car buyer from doing their job in the transaction.

I was talking with an acquaintance that was driving an expensive new car. I commented on how nice the car was, and she responded by describing the "deal" she had received. She mentioned how the salesman asked how much of a payment she was making on the car she was trading in, a much lesser automobile. Sure enough, the salesman quickly closed the deal by telling her she could drive away in the new car for the same monthly payment she was making on the old car. As you might guess, she was making loan payments on the trade-in but lease payments on the new car; that gave her the impression that the new car was a great deal.

I am not going to insult professional buyers and sellers by describing a new car transaction as an analogy of what could happen in a healthy customer-supplier partnership, but only to offer some insight regarding how a customer should be well-prepared before entering into a potential VMI commitment to a supplier.

With the monthly payment in hand, the salesman can now sell the buyer on the payment rather than the price. With the true cost of the car now obscured from vision through a focus on monthly payments, the interest rate, the length of the loan, a lease alternative, and the trade-in value can all be manipulated to trigger the buyer to close the deal.

We all know how the buyer could have retained control in this negotiation. First, they would state that they will purchase or lease the car based upon the fair value of the car and not monthly payments, and second, they would say that they want to agree on that fair value independent of the trade-in. They would then negotiate how much they would get for the trade, what interest rates, payment terms, and lease options were offered, and make their decision based solely on the elements of the cost of the transaction. They would also make sure that the trade-in was cleaned up and in good running condition before being assessed by the dealership, and they would already know the retail and trade-in value of their car from sources available on the internet.

Vendor Managed Inventory should only be considered after sufficient internal controls have been put in place to minimize Total Cost of Ownership. Your Lean TCO Program team will not be able to accurately assess VMI alternatives if your cost basis has not been reduced. If you are going to "trade in" your internal control for supplier control, make sure your trade-in is looking its best. Many new car sales are lost when the potential buyer shines up their trade in and then decides that their current ride is just fine after all.

Before leaving the topic of Vendor Managed Inventory, I need to share one story from years ago. We had a customer that was using an outside service to stock first aid cabinets. We were providing a variety of safety products to the facility and the buyer asked if we would be interested providing first aid products as well. Anxious to increase sales, I agreed to install 8 new first aid cabinets and provide the cabinet stocking VMI service. Sizable facilities can spend upwards of $500 a month for vendor managed first aid supplies, so I thought it might be a good area of business to get into. I installed and stocked the first aid cabinets and then returned the following month. A few miscellaneous items were all that was needed, less than $10.00 in first aid products. The following month I had the same experience and invoiced again for a very small amount. By the fourth month I finally broke the $20.00 barrier. Having invested *over 10 times* my *revenue* in my four monthly visits, I had to let the customer know that I could no longer afford to provide the service. I was certainly not willing to start randomly invoicing my customer $200 to $300 due to my expenses. Since that time, we have had a number of customers switch out of first aid VMI provided by other suppliers and stock their own first aid cabinets, all saving hundreds of dollars per month.

Before pursuing a VMI solution, ask yourself these questions:

> "If we had *effective and efficient control* of our supply item inventory, and if our prices paid were highly competitive, what specific gains would my company experience with a VMI solution?"

> "Would those potential gains offset the risk of turning over that *effective and efficient control* to a 3rd party?"

One last poke at VMI. I have heard from many buyers how much they like dealing with vendors who manage the inventory they supply. Who can blame them. If they receive a competitive quote and don't have to do as much work, they are naturally going to be attracted to VMI offerings. This is particularly true when the buyer has other more important and more pressing job responsibilities. In the context of lean analysis, *none of these considerations apply* unless the lean analysis has determined otherwise. The workload of the buyer and apparently competitive pricing might justify a *traditional* purchase decision, but they are not sufficient to justify a more progressive *lean* purchase decision.

Vending Machines

Vending solutions for supply items are rapidly expanding. Vending machines can now dispense almost any type of supply item and they offer a variety of potential benefits to customers. Vending machines are expensive; the cost of the machines and the cost of restocking must be considered regardless of whether or not a supplier is covering some or all of those costs within the prices paid for the vended items.

At a minimum, a vending machine can provide point-of-use inventory to minimize how far employees have to walk to obtain supply items while also providing some protection of inventory to help reduce shrinkage. Vending machines can be equipped with technology that allows item-level and employee-level tracking of supply usage. For example, if there are 5 production departments that each have their own vending machines for supplies, data on how much supply inventory is consumed by each department and each employee can be gathered. This type of data can be very useful in controlling spend through the ability to analyze the data for excessive usage patterns. If the employee must identify themselves through the entry of an employee identification code (whether by keypad, swiping a badge, or other means), there is also the benefit that employees will know that their vending transactions are being tracked. This will reduce excess use by encouraging employees to exercise discipline. They are less likely to replace items prematurely, such as a pair of work gloves that are still of good use, and they are more likely to keep track of the items they are responsible for.

Under certain circumstances, some employers will even charge their employees for items obtained from vending machines. For example, when employees are initially provided with the supply items they need, they might be charged if they prematurely replace those items because they have been lost or damaged. Some vending solutions also include the ability to identify which items each employee is authorized to obtain and will not dispense any unauthorized items.

In advanced applications, vending machines can communicate over the internet with suppliers that keep them stocked, letting suppliers know inventory levels and consumption rates for each item and when items reach a restocking point. Suppliers can respond without notification from the customer, eliminating all corresponding internal expenses.

There are a number of concerns associated with vending solutions. First, inventory changes can be expensive to implement and supply item usage can be inherently unstable. Item changes, new items, and discontinued items not only require changing out the vended items, they can also result in the need for substantial changes in vending equipment configuration. Changes to supply items that might otherwise reduce TCO could be mitigated by the need to deal with corresponding vending machine issues. Second, changes in usage levels can be difficult to manage. This can be a significant concern if installed vending machines present a capacity limitation. Third, when suppliers are responsible for stocking vending machines and supplier performance issues arise, there can be considerable expense and time delay in resolving those issues. Finally, depending upon restocking frequency, the cost of refilling vending machines could be excessive. This is a greater concern if the restocking is performed by a supplier that must frequently travel to the facility to provide the service.

If an organization's primary interest in vending solutions is to have point-of-use supply item availability, there are less expensive alternatives to consider. Cabinets, rather than vending machines, can provide point-of-use access with substantially less expense. Cabinets can be left unlocked in applications where shrinkage and excessive supply usage are not concerns. Locked cabinets can otherwise be used, but it is important to recognize the corresponding costs of controlling employee access. If an employee needs to locate a supervisor to gain access to a supply item, there are potentially substantial overhead and productivity costs associated with that supply item transaction.

There are manufacturers of locks that use Radio Frequency Identification (RFID) technology. Keys to open these locks have self-identifying circuitry so that access can be controlled and monitored. Unlike mechanical locks, these electronic locks can identify who has accessed a supply cabinet and when. This technology does not provide the same level of security as vending machines that monitor every item dispensed, but it may be a viable alternative for your facility.

Although many of the benefits of vending machines can be gained by other less expensive methods, and although vending machines induce their own TCO components that must be offset by other savings, they may still represent your best alternative for certain commodities depending upon the specific needs of your facility and the capabilities of your suppliers.

Inventory Consignment

Typically combined with Vendor Managed Inventory solutions, Inventory Consignment involves a supplier who provides supply inventory at the customer's facility without requiring the customer to pay for that inventory until it is pulled from a stocking location or a vending machine.

The customer can benefit in two ways. First and most obviously, there is supply inventory available directly to supply users that has not yet been purchased. This can reduce or eliminate the inventory carrying cost component of TCO. Second, depending upon the nature of the consignment agreement, the risk of dead inventory is eliminated for any consigned supply items that become obsolete.

Referring to Chapter 6 where we discuss the importance of cost control over cost diversion, and again mentioning the criticality of supplier partnerships that reduce mutual costs, consignment agreements should only be pursued after an open discussion between the customer and supplier about the risks and benefits to both parties. Chapter 6 also discusses the importance of aligning responsibilities within the partnership in accordance with which party has control over corresponding costs. If not implemented carefully, inventory consignment can shift the cost of poor inventory management from the customer to the supplier and mitigate the opportunity for the partnership to resolve the underlying issues.

Finally, supply related inventory carrying costs tend to be a very small component of TCO. This means that even if inventory consignment is implemented in an ideal fashion, the resulting benefit to the customer might not be substantial.

Consider all of the various "calling plans" offered by wireless telephone service providers. Free minutes, unused minutes that roll over to the next billing period, free calls to your family, free calls to your friends... marketers try all of these "benefits" in order to find the one that triggers you to select their plan. Don't let a consigned inventory offering be that kind of a trigger; instead, work out a consigned inventory agreement with your supplier partner only if that is the best arrangement for the partnership.

Reverse Auctions

Nothing screams "I buy based on price" louder than reverse auctions. Since I *am* a strong advocate of partnerships, I *am not* a strong advocate of reverse auctions.

If you have ever bought or sold an item on an online auction site, you might have experienced a bit of a rush as the auction came to a close. I received a call from Ben, a good friend, who asked "Do you want to go on a road trip?" I replied "Sure! Where and when?" He said "Syracuse, this weekend, if I win this auction on a boat up there." I had never used online auctions and I asked him how the auction process worked. He explained it to me and then showed me how I could watch the live bidding activity on the boat as the auction closed.

I was up for the trip, even though it was a 14 hour drive from Nashville. Ben, an entrepreneur himself, is not only a good friend but a great sounding-board when it comes to talking business. I knew we would have some fun on the trip and that I would get plenty of free expert advice... so I watched the end of the auction with some anticipation. In a flurry of last moment bids, Ben won and we were off to Syracuse. Ben is a self-proclaimed online auction expert, and he called again a year or two later to say he was looking at a Jaguar in Cleveland. That was a "one-way road trip"; we flew to Cleveland to drive his prize back to Nashville. I'm still waiting for Ben to win an auction where the item we need to fetch is in a tropical destination.

I have been involved in Federal reverse auctions in my supply business. We have won a few bids and we don't mind the occasional bump in sales, but our margins are always dismal at best. It takes a large bid to get our interest. Federal reverse auctions are the ultimate in bottom-dollar pricing, but are they truly effective at minimizing Total Cost of Ownership?

Reverse auctions can be expensive to set up and manage even with the use of internet technology. Depending upon the size of the purchase, the cost involved with executing the auction may be excessive with respect to prices paid. The more important consideration is that reverse auctions would be difficult, if not impossible, to integrate into Lean TCO processes that involve strategic supplier partnerships. They are likely to produce an excessive number of purchases with substantial overhead costs.

Procurement Business Process Outsourcing

Business Process Outsourcing (BPO) is gaining in popularity and can be applied to almost any business function… including procurement. BPO is an area of business services where the BPO service provider acts as a third party to perform an outsourced business function on behalf of the customer. The core concept behind BPO is efficiency of scale, where a third party is able to leverage a focused area of expertise across multiple customers and achieve performance results that are better than those that customers could achieve on their own. With Procurement BPO, there is also the potential for third party buying power advantages to reduce prices paid as well as overhead costs.

As good as this may sound on the surface, the customer must always remember that any outsourced service, whether within a simple VMI relationship or a complex BPO relationship, carries with it a profit margin for the service provider that the customer must pay for. The customer must also remember that the degree of control that is lost in an outsourced relationship can sometimes lead to effects opposite of the goal to substantially decrease TCO.

This book is not written to advocate any particular solution, but to build customer-supplier partnerships that achieve dramatic reductions in TCO. It is up to the customer to apply the strategies, tools, and techniques described in this book to select the right partners with the right products and services. Procurement contracts, VMI solutions, and procurement BPO solutions all carry the risk that comes with the customer giving up some degree of control, and that risk must be outweighed by the benefits of those arrangements.

We clearly do not advocate the pursuit of any binding relationship with any supplier or outsourcing service provider until a sufficient level of internal control has been established. If the customer acknowledges that TCO is excessive and that supply management is in need of a complete overhaul, it is never advisable for the customer to "throw over the fence" anything in a state of disarray for another organization to fix.

Earlier in this chapter, I discussed a new car transaction between a car buyer and a new car salesman. I emphasize the importance of the car buyer remaining focused on the fair value of the car without being manipulated by the salesman when it comes to financing options, leasing options, and the value of the buyer's trade-in. Those same ideas apply to Procurement BPO.

Before entering into any binding contract with a supplier, the customer has to be in a position to know real costs and must have supply management under sufficient control to be able to accurately evaluate those costs. It can be very tempting to jump into a Procurement BPO arrangement when the numbers on the surface appear attractive, just like many car buyers jump behind the wheel when they decide they can afford the monthly payment they were sold on. The customer can't know if they are getting the right deal without understanding exactly what the external solution offers in comparison to already-streamlined internal operations.

In the final analysis, the operational efficiency and buying power of the service provider must be large enough to offset the profit margin they need to achieve. Furthermore, the customer needs evidence that service will not only be excellent at the onset of the agreement, but will be sustained throughout the term of the agreement regardless of countervailing influences within the service provider. Those negative influences could be related to any number of factors, including personnel issues, financial issues, changes in corporate direction, and so on.

It can be challenging enough for a customer to manage the performance of their own employees; if a contracted service provider is failing to perform due to their own internal personnel issues, the customer cannot directly impact that performance. Don't turn to contracts that contain strong language about maintaining service levels as the answer... if personnel performance issues that affect all organizations could be fixed with a few words in a contractual document, those hundreds of books giving advice on how to manage employee performance would not be in print.

Another key consideration for Procurement BPO and VMI involves the frequent need for immediate support. Due to the nature of consumable supplies, no matter how well they are controlled, urgent needs will arise. When they do, the customer will need to have access to the service provider's personnel that can immediately research, source, and supply an item. A lack of immediate support could lead to substantial costs within the customer's organization. Even if the contract allows the customer to purchase outside of the agreement under certain conditions, the value of the contract is mitigated if the customer still needs to perform this type of work.

Suppliers: Time for a Gut Check

If you are a supplier, after reading up to this point in the book, you might have a few concerns about partnering with your customers to drive down TCO.   You might reasonably question your organization's ability to truly help with implementing a Lean TCO Program. If you are reading this book because a customer has asked you to, you should be ready to get to work quickly. If you are reading this book on your own, we are not suggesting that you immediately encourage your customers to do the same.   Although we would appreciate the book sales, if you are not well-prepared, they could quickly determine that you are no longer their most suitable supplier.

We are providing the framework to produce enduring customer-supplier partnerships for mutual financial benefit, and within that context, we suggest that you take a hard inward look at your business methods so that you can make the changes that would compel your customers not only to partner with you in a Lean TCO Program, but to expand their business with you in the process. You must also take an outward look at your customer's methods of procuring and handling supply items. The more you understand your customer, the better able you will be to support their needs and also make recommendations on how your partnership with them could substantially reduce costs.

Know Your Supply Procurement Options

121

Chapter 5

Free Freight and Other Supply Chain Myths

There is no such thing as free freight. Not only does someone within the supply chain have to pay for freight, it is ultimately paid for by you, the customer. Not only do you pay for the freight to your facility, you pay for all freight from the manufacturer's dock to your supplier's warehouse. Not only do you pay the cost of transportation, you pay for the profit each freight carrier earns along the way. At the risk of offending some readers, I will be blunt about this point. If a seller buries the cost of freight or delivery in prices paid, it should be insulting to the buyer when the seller says it is free. If anyone out there knows of a company that manufacturers trucks and gives them away for free, a company that maintains trucks for free, gas stations that offer free fuel, and drivers that prefer not to receive a paycheck... my contact information is in the back of this book. I will spread the word and generate a tremendous amount of business for them.

So what other supply-related "free" services does your organization pay for? The short answer... all of them. You are paying for whatever your supply base is doing for free regardless of what the invoice says. Unless, of course, the supplier does not have a sustainable business model. Are there exceptions? Sure, but only if what is being provided for free is temporary and not a part of the supplier's normal business practices. If it is in their normal business practices for no charge, then *it is in prices paid.*

An experienced procurement executive I know attended a presentation for a Vendor Managed Inventory solution that included "free" vending machines for industrial supplies. He asked the presenter a simple question: "How to you amortize (pay for) the expense of the vending machines you put in my facility?" The paraphrased answer was: "You don't have to worry about that because they are free." The procurement professional did not buy the answer... and did not buy the solution.

Buyers reading this book who utilize free supplier services might be thinking "wait a minute, my prices paid with the supplier offering free services are competitive." To be fair to those readers, I will argue the one case where use of the term "free" can be used without causing me excessive indigestion (although it still causes me some). That case is when order volumes are sufficient enough to have a measurable impact on *efficiencies internal to the supplier.*

The most common example is when a customer meets an order minimum that allows the supplier sufficient profit to not put a line item on the invoice for freight. Notice how carefully I worded the previous sentence... I did not say that the supplier pays for the freight. You as the customer are still paying for the freight within prices paid, but your order is large enough that the supplier does not *charge you more* for freight than they are already charging within their product pricing. The supplier can do this when internal operating costs and shipping costs are spread out over larger dollar purchases. Processing an order for $100 in product involves a much higher percentage of overhead when compared to processing an order for a $2000 purchase.

Consider the late-night commercials for products where the pitch man is saying (or yelling) "If you call now, we will give you the second one for free!" Do you rush to the phone to get the "free" product? If you do, you will need a lot more than this book to help you. Of course you don't rush to the phone. You're already insulted by the pitch man who is thinking you just might be that gullible.

The traditional argument for presenting and accepting free services is a simple one, even without order minimums. If the buyer likes the price and gets the corresponding service for free, and if the seller makes sufficient margin at that price to cover the cost of the service, an agreement is reached and the business relationship moves forward. So what is the problem with this scenario?

Free Services Hide Costs

Let's take a look at how the offer of "free" services can obscure the root causes of excessive TCO, not allowing them to be visible to the customer-supplier partnership. We will demonstrate this through a simple example of how free services can eliminate the opportunity for the customer to work with the supplier in reducing or eliminating underlying costs.

Consider free delivery offered by a local suppler, a common practice by sellers that allows buyers to make purchase decisions without concern for shipping charges. The exchange between the buyer and seller might go something like this:

> **Buyer:** "Your prices look competitive, you have a good reputation, and I like that you are local. Do you offer free delivery?"
>
> **Seller:** "Can you tell me how much your typical order might be?"
>
> **Buyer:** "We spend about $1500 per month in this product category and I like to place orders once every two weeks."
>
> **Seller:** "Sounds great. We already have other accounts nearby, so that helps. What if we set up an order minimum for free delivery?"
>
> **Buyer:** "I'm very busy and don't want to worry about whether or not my orders add up to a minimum requirement. It would also be hard to figure out what I

should add to an order to reach an order minimum. My other local suppliers don't require minimums."

Seller: "No problem. We'll waive the order minimum."

The buyer is satisfied since they know there will not be any expense other than the purchase price. The seller is satisfied since they anticipate the ability to deliver to multiple nearby accounts at one time and expects to be delivering about $750 in product per order to this new account.

The business relationship gets started and the new supplier begins to receive orders from their new account. The orders are more frequent than one every two weeks, and even though the new account is generating the expected revenue, the cost of delivery is high. Furthermore, many of the deliveries are rush orders and the supplier does not have the opportunity to coordinate delivery schedules with other customers near the new account. The supplier's internal personnel know that the new account has been set up with free delivery and no minimums, so no questions are asked.

It may appear on the surface that the customer is on the winning side of this new relationship. They have some internal supply control issues that result in frequent, small-dollar rush orders, and the supplier is happy to have the new account and they are responsive to every order placed. The supplier is even absorbing the cost of rush deliveries from their own product sources to support the new account, and for now, those costs are not being transferred to the customer.

At some point in the future, account review activity at the supplier may or may not reveal the cost concerns with the new account. The seller may or may not attempt upwardly adjust pricing to help cover the unexpected costs. For the sake of our example, we will assume that there is no upward price adjustment and the customer continues to enjoy pricing far below what they should otherwise pay.

Has the customer minimized Total Cost of Ownership in this scenario? Great pricing... great service... no delivery expense... and a supplier that is not pushing back. The buyer might even get some praise if the new supplier is providing product at lower prices than the previous supplier.

Here are the issues with this new relationship:

> **Issue #1:** Procurement professionals do not seek one-sided relationships, but partnerships that benefit the seller as well.

> **Issue #2:** The buyer is seeking cost diversion rather than cost control. Frequent orders produce costs within the new relationship that are the caused by the customer and diverted to the supplier.

> **Issue #3:** This relationship cannot endure. The supplier's service levels could drop as they become frustrated with the account, the supplier could attempt to raise prices, or worse, the supplier could go out of business if their inability to control costs is widespread across their customer base.

Issue #4: The buyer may have established a narrow source of supply; $1500 per month from a single supplier could indicate that the customer has an excessive number of suppliers.

Issue #5: Frequent orders and rush orders reflect tremendous internal costs. Those costs may also include production down-time if stock outs are involved. With the new supplier remaining silent and supportive, the customer is not working to reduce their substantial internal costs.

Issue #6: Supply chain costs that have dramatically escalated are not made readily visible to the customer and supplier; they are masked within the context of a free delivery relationship.

We will focus on Issue #6. Contrast the buyer-seller discussion presented previously with a buyer-seller discussion containing some straightforward dialogue:

Buyer: "Your prices look competitive, you have a good reputation, and you have a broad product offering. Tell me how you cover the cost of delivering product to my facility."

Seller: "As you know, the larger your orders, the lower our delivery costs as a percentage of our sales. Some of our customers prefer we cover our delivery costs within our prices, and others prefer a separate line item for delivery charges on our invoices."

Buyer: "If I chose to pay for delivery within the prices you charge, how do I benefit from providing you with larger, consolidated orders?"

Seller: "That is why we recommend a separate delivery charge regardless of the order size. Your prices would be the lowest we offer since we don't have to build in the risk of high overhead with small orders, and you can see for yourself from each invoice how much you are benefiting from order consolidation.

Buyer: "Sounds good, but I am concerned about how frequently I might have to place orders. We don't have the level of control I would like when in comes to our supply inventory, and I have to place a lot of rush orders.

Seller: "You're not alone. Many of our customers have those same challenges."

Buyer: "Let me give this some thought and get back to you."

Seller: "I look forward to your call."

In this scenario, the buyer is challenged to consider how well their inventory is managed and how easy it will be to consolidate orders. The buyer recognizes that rush orders will be a problem. It would have been much easier for the buyer to avoid the internal concerns buy negotiating a free delivery relationship, but without free delivery, the buyer (and management) is more motivated to get internal control issues addressed. It would have been much easier for the seller to "go for the close" and offer free delivery at their lowest prices, but the seller would be incurring the risk of excessive overhead.

I advocate the type of open and honest dialogue represented by the second conversation where the word *free* is not used for a *quick close*. Many books on sales techniques provide methods that salespeople use to "overcome objections" and close the sale. The first conversation is an example of that sales mentality. When the salesperson returns to the office and is asked about the meeting with the prospective customer, they are able to say that they closed the deal. In the second conversation, the salesperson would return to the office and say that the prospective customer may or may not be a good fit… a much less attractive result to present to the boss… but a better result nonetheless. The second conversation may lead to a partnership attitude between the customer and supplier where mutual costs are assessed and reduced to the substantial benefit of both parties.

Is That Your Supply Chain or a Flight Map?

Freight can be so ravaging to Total Cost of Ownership that it justifies a separate section in this book. Freight not only represents potentially substantial cost as product travels within the channel, cost is incurred in receiving, stocking, and pulling the product at each channel destination. As we just discussed, the customer pays for all of that activity with an additional profit to those that are performing that work.

Speaking of work, try not to roll your eyes as I put this in engineering terms. I have a Master's degree in Mechanical Engineering so just deal with it for a moment. Work is a measure of how much force is applied to an object to move it a certain distance:

$$Work = Force \times Distance$$

Think of the Force in that equation as "pushing" your supply item as it travels from the manufacturer's dock to your receiving dock. That "pushing" will include various forms of transportation, such as ocean freighters and 18 wheelers. It will also include fork lifts and human handling. Think of Distance in that equation, as, well, distance. How far does the product need to be "pushed" until it arrives at your dock? How many times? How direct is the path to your dock? So the Work performed on your supply item, all of which you pay for, is a measure of how hard and how far that product is pushed through the supply chain. Add a little paper "work" along the way and you have a lot of expense.

Consider the paths that your supply items typically follow as they travel from manufacturers through the supply chain and ultimately arrive at your facility. These paths could look like a flight map for a major international airline. Each path and each destination represents cost in the channel. The supplier must incur all of the costs that bring the product to their location. Large suppliers may also have transportation expenses between their own warehouses and retail locations. When the product is transferred to the customer, so is all of that cost incurred throughout the supply chain. Like customers, suppliers commonly have free freight options for acquiring their inventory, so the masking of real freight costs can occur within all of those paths between the manufacturer and the end-customer.

Consider a product manufactured in China that is ultimately going to be delivered to a customer in Denver. The item has to travel from the manufacturer to a port in China, likely incurring at least one trip to an inland freight terminal where it is combined with other products heading for the port. It travels by cargo ship to a port in the U. S., and from there it potentially travels to a freight terminal before being shipped to the manufacturer's U.S. warehouse. The product must then travel to the supplier's location. If the supplier has a central warehouse that supports multiple locations, the product might travel from the central warehouse to the supplier's Denver location. The product must then travel from the supplier's location to the end-customer's location. All of that assumes that the product is following a relatively direct path from the manufacturer to the customer, not being transferred more than once between supplier locations... or between different suppliers for that matter.

The Red Carpet Treatment

So what is more expensive? An ocean freighter traveling 3000 miles or a supplier delivery truck traveling 5 miles?

Imagine a box of a particular supply item heading to your location. We'll say that the box contains 6 dozen pairs of work gloves and weighs 35 pounds. Starting with the manufacturing plant in China, a full size freight container is filled with the various gloves they produce. In the container is a particular skid of gloves, and on that skid is our box of 6 dozen pairs.

Back to Work equals Force times Distance. When that box is being moved within the container by the ocean freighter, the ship's captain doesn't have to adjust the throttle to handle the additional load of your 35 pound box. Zero force times 3000 miles across the ocean equals zero Work. Our box is barely distinguishable within the freight container full of gloves; the presence of our box goes completely unnoticed on the cargo ship that contains thousands of freight containers. (At the time of the writing of this book, the world's largest freight container ship carries over 15,000 containers.) Additionally, the ship is traveling between ports regardless our box. That ship is sailing with or without our 35 pounds of cargo.

The cost of the ocean freighter isn't quite zero, but it is close. What about the last leg of the journey, when your box is on your supplier's delivery truck? That box is now receiving some very personal attention. A few weeks ago it could not be distinguished from hundreds of thousands of other boxes on the ocean freighter; now it is being driven around by a chauffer in a limousine.

Whenever a supplier makes a local delivery, I want your Lean TCO Program team to have a clear picture of the corresponding costs. Your box of gloves, having watched some satellite TV in the limo while sipping champagne, arrives. The red carpet has been rolled out in your receiving area. The chauffer not only opens the limo door for the box of gloves, he escorts the gloves down the red carpet. With cameras flashing, your doorman then ushers the chauffer and your box of work gloves into your facility.

Other less important boxes might be dropped off by the busload and hustled through your Receiving Department without any fanfare, but not this box. The chauffer presents the box to the waiting admirers and even lingers for a period of time. If the chauffer is particularly friendly, he may linger for over an hour as he arranges an opportunity for another box to attend another event at your facility in the near future.

It is that last leg of the journey, the last few miles out of thousands of miles, that is so extremely expensive. Our streets are littered with supplier delivery vehicles, each hustling around carrying tiny amounts of product to their destinations, with all of those products enjoying the red carpet treatment.

The point is this. Supply items moved simultaneously in substantially large volumes incur substantially less cost per item. I encourage you to take a look at how many invoices your organization has received over the past year for consumable supply orders of less than $500.

I was at a customer location in their receiving area when a truck backed into the loading dock. Within a few minutes, two skids were removed from the truck, a Bill of Lading was signed, and the truck was gone. The shrink wrap that was holding tall, miscellaneous assortments of boxes on the skids was removed, and a Receiving Clerk was verifying the shipment against a packing list. It wasn't long before the supply inventory on the skids was going into stocking locations in the warehouse. What struck me was the fact that the whole process did not take much longer than it would have if one box was received; the Receiving Clerk jumped to action as the dock door was being opened. The lean wheels in my mind were turning. Perhaps there were $3000 in supply items on those two skids, received and stocked in less than 30 minutes.

$3000 of supplies divided by 30 minutes
equals $100.00 in supplies received per minute

That Receiving Department was getting a broad variety of supply items received and into warehouse locations at an estimated rate of $100.00 in product every 60 seconds. Let's compare that to the chauffer-delivered box of $25.00 in work gloves.

Chauffer: Good to see you Steve. Here are the gloves. We appreciate the business.

Steve: Thanks for bring them over Jim.

Chauffer: Hey, how about those Colts. Indianapolis is looking good again this year.

Steve: They need a little work on defense, don't you think?

Chauffer: …

Steve: …

-
-
-
-

Chauffer: Is Debbie around today?

Steve: I think so, let me check (dialing the phone). Hi Debbie, Jim's here, he's on his way up.

Chauffer: (Walking through the offices) Hey Nick. How are the wife and kids?

Nick: They're doing great, Jim. How's your family?

Chauffer: …

Nick: …

-

-
-
-

Chauffer: (Still walking through the offices) Hey Janice. Congrats on the big promotion. Nick was just telling me about it.

Janice: I'm working 60 hours a week just trying to keep up.

Chauffer: …

Janice: …

-
-
-
-
-

Chauffer: (Finally to Debbie's office) Hi Debbie, thought I would stop in and see if you need anything. I just got the gloves to Steve.

Debbie: Thanks for the great service, Jim. We really needed those gloves.

Chauffer: Is there anything else I can help you with right now?

Debbie: Maintenance called and said they need some extension cords. You guys sell those?

Chauffer: Sure do. I've got our catalog right here. Let's call Maintenance and pick something out; I'll be back with what you need. How about this weather? I'm not ready for winter yet.

Debbie: Neither am I. I just had to cover all of my flowers because of that early frost last night.

Chauffer: ...

Debbie: ...

-
-
-
-

Let's do the math on this delivery:

$25 of supplies divided by 60 minutes
equals 42 cents in supplies received per minute

Compared to the 2 skids with $3000 in product, the rate of receiving expense for the gloves is 240 times greater. To some this example will seem a little over-stated, to others it will appear painfully familiar. We'll carry these numbers to a ridiculous extreme just to make a point. If organization A's supplies were always received $3000 at a time from a common carrier, and if organization B's supplies were always delivered by friendly and talkative local suppliers $25.00 at a time, and both organizations purchased the same supplies, how would their staffing requirements compare? Organization B would require over 200 times the manpower to receive supply items when compared to Organization A.

It is obvious that no organization is at the second extreme, but our little bit of fun with the numbers does reveal that there may be significant value in receiving larger amounts of supply items by common carrier as opposed to smaller amounts of supply items by supplier delivery vehicle.

I would like your Lean TCO Program team to visualize every supplier that appears at your facility with a small order as a chauffer in a tux... white gloves and all.

A true appreciation for real supply chain costs must also include the amount of time the product sits in a warehouse location. I hope I have already convinced you that freight isn't free. The same applies to inventory warehousing. Your Lean TCO Program team needs to understand all supply chain costs... all of the costs that occur within the channel as product travels from the manufacturer's shipping dock to your receiving dock. They will need to work on internal processes and with your suppliers to accomplish the following:

- Minimizing the number of times product must move within the channel

- Maximizing the quantity of product moved any time movement within the channel is required

- Minimizing how long product resides at any location within the channel

They will also need to counsel suppliers when they throw the "free" word around. As discussed in detail in Chapter 6, this book encourages the formation of strategic partnerships with your suppliers where the partnership seeks to minimize mutual costs in order to share in the corresponding benefits. Your team will need your supplier's costs out in the open. When a cost is hiding behind "free", it is much harder to put it in the cross-hairs and pull the trigger.

Know What You're Paying For

Manufacturers work hard to avoid having their products perceived as commodity items. Most manufacturers use some combination of innovation, marketing, branding, packaging, promotional activity, and restricted distribution in an effort to maintain or improve product margins.

We are certainly not against branding and marketing, I have done plenty of branding and marketing work in my own businesses. As consumers, we can often distinguish between the hype and the substance and make good purchases. At the same time, we can also fall prey to the hype and make a purchase that we regret when we learn that the product or service does not live up to what was advertised.

When it comes to commodity products (which virtually all consumable supplies are), manufacturers try to distinguish themselves and their products in order to increase the sense of value in the eyes of the person who will potentially select their product over a large number of competitive alternatives. That value may be real; the manufacturer may have true innovation in their product that deserves the attention of the buyer. The manufacturer may also be protecting their brand through a true commitment to product quality. Manufacturers that consistently produce high quality, dependable supply items are clearly deserving of higher prices than those who don't. It is reasonable for a buyer to be persuaded by a brand that consistently delivers high quality. Unfortunately, buyers are often persuaded to pay more for well branded products than the products themselves merit.

Working as a supplier of commodity items, buyers new to our supply business would often have a number of well branded items that we would change over to lesser-recognized brands that still fit the buyer's application. Dramatic reductions in prices paid can occur under these circumstances. Previous suppliers may have guided the buyer to more expensive products. For the same reason as manufacturers, suppliers often try to market higher priced commodity items that can produce higher revenues and higher margins.

I believe that it is the job of the supplier to *embrace the commodity nature* of their business and offer their customers the lowest cost product that meets the needs of the application. The supplier acting as a true partner will not pursue higher revenue or higher margin product alternatives and will not align themselves with well branded manufacturers that offer no price or feature benefit. The supplier acting as a true partner will filter out the meaningless promotional, marketing, or not-so-innovative new products on behalf of their customers and will work hard to keep commodity item prices where they should be… extremely low.

Chapter 6

Redefine Your Customer-Supplier Partnerships

When I first began recruiting engineering talent as a young manager, I was taught that it was best to get out from behind my desk and sit on the other side with the candidate during interviews. The concept was not only to put the candidate a little more at ease, but to demonstrate the idea that recruiting was not a negotiation but an attempt to find the right employer-employee partnership. The candidate was potentially interested in the job and I was interested in getting the corresponding work output of that position; but what was more important than the job, the salary, and the work output was the fit between candidate and employer.

The last thing the candidate should ask is how much the job pays, just as the manager should not start the interview with a discussion of potential compensation. The candidate might have a salary target in mind and the manager might have budgetary limitations, but if the fit is right, the money issues are likely to get worked out. Conversely, if the fit is wrong, there was never any point in talking about money to begin with.

Having hired hundreds of employees over my career, without hesitation I can say that fit is so important that money (within reason) is nearly inconsequential. When I was not hiring for my own business but for an employer, I would justify to Human Resources that pushing the envelope of a pay grade was justified by the factors that made the candidate an ideal fit for the organization. The analogy is obvious. Selecting suppliers based upon price alone would be like selecting employees based upon their income requirements alone. Imagine this classified add:

> "Seeking a Vice President of Operations. Will fill the position with the lowest bidder."

Everyone in the corporation, except perhaps for the President, would be working for minimum wage.

When strategically sourcing your supply items, prices certainly do matter. They are important as a hard, easily measured component of TCO. They are also important as they may reflect upon the supplier's operating efficiencies. High prices may indicate high levels of inefficiency or high cost business models. High prices may also reflect issues of supplier integrity. If prices with a current supplier are competitive, but not necessarily the most competitive, that supplier should remain on your list of potential strategic partners.

A Word About Relationships

Ask yourself this question: "When should a salesman know the name of a buyer's daughter?" Let that sink in for a minute and then check an answer below.

__ when the buyer is still a prospect

__ after the buyer has made a purchase

__ never

I hope you struggled to make a selection. I purposely left out what I consider to be the only reasonable answer: *maybe* after the buyer and seller have enjoyed a mutually beneficial, professional relationship for some period of time.

Salespeople are typically well trained. Many have been through numerous books and seminars in order to fine tune their approach, appearance, and style. Many have been trained to come across as comfortable and relaxed so that their training in approach, appearance, and style comes out naturally. Not only are they equipped with knowledge of the products and services they offer, they are equipped with tools to get to the decision maker and then to get the desired decision. If you are a decision maker, you are a means to an end for the salesperson.

This may sound harsh, but it is reality. Salespeople with the highest level of ethical conduct, all of those we know and enjoy doing business with, have the same job to do as those of lesser character… to get decision makers to buy from their company. The challenge for decision makers is to remain focused on the needs of their organization, and unfortunately, that has absolutely nothing to do with the approach, appearance, style, and likeability of the salesperson. It may, though, have everything to do with the character of the salesperson. The character of the supplier's salesperson might be a strong reflection of the character of the supplier.

You might be thinking, "this guy hates salesmen." Not true. I do hate, though, the very idea of being sold. So should you. As a rational human being that can analyze options, I just need the *facts* on my *options*. The last thing I need is to be *sold* on the *facts* on my *options*. If I am buying a house, I don't need the realtor telling me that "the schools are great", I need the realtor providing the facts about how the students in the school test against national averages.

Some of you might be thinking about salespeople you know who say that they try to find the right match between a prospective customer's organization and their own. They might claim that they don't want to "sell" you, but only to work with you to determine if a good match exists. That too is a sales tactic that has been written about in many books on selling.

Do we sell? Sure. Visit www.LeanTCO.com, do some clicking around, and let us know if you're interested in seminars, consulting services, Supply Control Systems, Restock Now, or MSDS Access. We'll talk about the facts of what we do and get you on our newsletter email list. That will be about it for our sales pitch. We would like to get to know you if we do some business together, but you won't have to prepare a list of your hobbies, interests, family member names, and favorite sports teams just to find out what we have to offer.

If you are a buyer, what would you do if a salesperson sat across from you and provided a series of facts related to his products or services, smiled, and left. The sad reality is that you probably would not buy his products or services regardless of how compelling the facts were. We are social creatures; we are relational. Our lives are largely defined by our relationships. This book is being written during the boom in on-line social networking... we can now connect to thousands of others by pressing a few buttons on a keypad. We do it because we like to feel connected and we like to interact.

Our human nature is fine when it comes to our buying choices with restaurants or hair stylists. Even if we make a "poor" value decision, that lack of value might be outweighed by enjoyable interaction with people we like. A likable waiter that provides good service and knows us by name can overcome an occasional disappointment with how our meal was prepared. When it comes to strategic sourcing decisions, however, our social nature is a liability that can prevent the formation of healthy supplier partnerships.

Don't get me wrong.   As a supplier, we have many great relationships with people who purchase and use our supply items and our services. We often know quite a bit about their families and may know some of the important things that are going on in their lives at any given time. We have a genuine interest in them as individuals, and one of the blessings of working closely with customers is the opportunity to enjoy new friendships. We would like to believe that all of these friendships were formed as a result of our service attitude; our belief in our responsibility to perform on behalf of our customers that reward us with business.

Regardless of those friendships, if one of those buyers determines that there is a better strategic sourcing option for their supplies, they have a far greater responsibility to their employer than they do to us. When we are making purchasing decisions as consumers, it can be logical to consider the likeability of the people on the other side of the transaction. This can be particularly important in consumer decisions that lead to ongoing interactions with the other party. A good friend of mine recently took a new job and had to upgrade his wardrobe. He visited a clothing store and received outstanding personal attention. He bought two suits and admitted he may have paid an extra $100 for each, but he placed a high value on the personal attention he received and anticipates that he will do ongoing business with that store. Based upon how highly he rated the personal attention, the next time I need a suit, I will probably go to that store.

If he were purchasing uniforms for his employer's workforce rather than a couple of suits for himself, his decision making process would have gone from highly appropriate to highly inappropriate. The likeability of the salesperson and the anticipation of future enjoyable interactions with that salesperson could never be a justifiable basis for causing his employer to spend more on the uniforms than they would otherwise need to. Regarding the personal interaction, his assessment would have to shift from likeability to integrity, from attentiveness to dependability, and from personal value to corporate value.

I hope my point is clear. Personal relationships should follow, not lead, business relationships. To many sales professionals, building relationships is considered to be the cornerstone of building new business. It usually is. When it comes to supply items, though, the likeability of a salesperson simply has nothing to do with Total Cost of Ownership and strategic partnerships.

Try this with the next salesperson who asks you personal questions *before* you conduct any business with them. Tell the salesperson that you raise llamas. It will be very hard for the salesperson to come up with a connection to that statement, and it might be fun to watch them try.

> "Well, umm, that sounds fascinating… I know
> someone, that, umm…"

Don't be surprised if you get a book on llamas from the salesperson, or some link in an email from the salesperson for an on-line network of llama owners. Perhaps you will get a small bronze llama from the salesperson to set on your desk as a reminder of their thoughtfulness... then your co-workers will come in and ask "what's with the llama?" and you'll have a great story to tell.

Negotiate Together Against Supply Chain Cost

To establish a powerful partnership that will minimize TCO, it is necessary to break away from the restrictions of the traditional customer-supplier relationship. To help define a true partnership, we will start with the idea that the supplier is a part of the customer's organization. Although this is not realistic for a number of reasons, including most fundamentally that customers cannot purchase the majority of their supply items directly from manufacturers and that distributors provide consolidated sourcing that makes freight and overhead manageable, it serves to establish a picture of what an ultimate partnership might look like.

If the supplier were a part of the customer's organization, the supplier could be called the "Supply Department" and would consist of buyers, customer service personnel, material handlers, and a warehouse. Note that there would be no salespeople. Corporate management would establish performance objectives for the Supply Department and would establish expectations for their facilities obtaining, controlling, and internally distributing supply items. Management would seek to assure supply availability at a minimum Total Cost of Ownership.

Using this model, there are no competitive conflicts. No member of this "supply chain" would seek to increase any cost to the corporation.

If this structure existed at a Six Sigma company, a team might be deployed to apply DMAIC methods to all processes involved. Highly efficient processes would be developed to manage supply inventory and obtain that inventory from the Supply Department. Those refined processes would virtually eliminate stock outs due to the team's clear understanding of corresponding process disruption and expense. Furthermore, those processes would function with a minimal amount of labor.

Management would require the Supply Department to operate within budgetary constraints. Management would require users of the supplies to manage their usage in a way that would reduce order frequency and eliminate rush orders, allowing the Supply Department to keep their expenses within budget.

Management would not want to incur any freight costs beyond the minimum necessary to keep the Supply Department and all facilities properly stocked. Management would seek to consolidate manufacturers and part numbers to control freight and maximize purchasing power.

The Supply Department would have substantial product knowledge and would assist the various supply users with product selection, product support, and problem resolution. Management would minimize the introduction of new supply items due to the disruptions new items would cause in the established system.

Management would want the Supply Department to remain on top of significant developments in the supply marketplace, but not waste the time of supply users with suggestions of new supply alternatives unless those alternatives would ultimately reduce TCO.

Finally, accountabilities would be established with the Supply Department and each facility in accordance with what is under their respective control. For example, the Supply Department would be accountable for incoming freight and efficient packaging of product for shipment, and the facilities would be held accountable for effective inventory control that minimizes freight related to frequent or rush shipments.

There wouldn't be any delivery vehicles traveling from the Supply Department to a facility due to the tremendous expense involved. Common carriers would be used for all shipments from the Supply Department and those shipments would involve large volumes of product. With the systems and accountabilities in place and clearly understood, measurements would be established to confirm that all parties are performing in a manner to meet or exceed TCO reduction objectives.

There are two fundamental conclusions to draw from the perspective established above:

1. The total cost incurred by both partners must be minimized in order to maximize the financial effectiveness of the partnership.

2. In order to minimize total costs, each financial accountability must be aligned with the partner who has control over that accountability.

The mindset of the supplier in this partnership has to shift from maximizing revenue and margin to minimizing cost. The mindset of the customer in this partnership has to shift from cost diversion to cost control (see the next section). If both the supplier and customer are successful in this change of mindset, the supplier can earn a fair profit with a very small operating margin and the customer can achieve the minimum TCO possible. Furthermore, an enduring partnership can be formed since each partner is managing the accountabilities that fall under their control... helping to improve mutual financial performance and avoiding the frustrations that misplaced accountabilities inevitably cause.

Both partners are now on the same side of the negotiating table... no longer negotiating against each other but together fighting against supply chain costs that contribute no value to either party.

Replace Cost Diversion with Cost Control

If your driving record is spotless… and even if you have been given a corresponding discount in your automobile insurance rate… your insurance premium is paying for those with lesser driving records. Compare this to suppliers that have offered customers free delivery without a minimum order requirement. A customer experiences a stock out and contacts that supplier to immediately bring over replacement inventory. They are not prepared to place a full stocking order, and the supplier responds with excellent service and drops off a $50.00 order. The supplier's margin on the supply item is $15.00, but $35.00 has been spent by the supplier in getting that rush order into their customer's hands. The net result of the transaction is a $20.00 loss for the supplier.

If the supplier offers free delivery with no minimums to a large number of accounts, and they experience profit loss with a number of deliveries to those accounts, their overall pricing structure has to cover those losses. The customers that frequently place low-dollar rush orders are diverting cost back into the supply chain, and the supply chain responds by transferring those costs back into the customer community… just like your insurance premiums that cover claims submitted by individuals other than yourself.

Cost diversion occurs upstream all the way through the supply chain, affecting manufacturers and all other supply chain participants.

Low dollar orders and rush orders have a substantial impact on freight, and in some cases, that excessive freight expense works its way back to the manufacturer. Suppliers that struggle to manage their own inventory attempt to divert costs in the same way as their customers who struggle with inventory management.

Are there other forms of cost diversion? Absolutely. A lack of effective item specification by the customer can lead to expensive inventory management challenges with their suppliers. This is particularly true when a supplier is maintaining an inventory of an item that no other customers purchase; a casual decision by the customer to switch from one item to another can induce substantial cost for the supplier. In the worst case scenario, the supplier cannot unload their inventory of the replaced item. Even if the customer has done reasonably well at supply item stability, inconsistent ordering patterns can have suppliers sitting on excess inventory or incurring expense when placing rush orders with their own sources. Supply item needs can be inherently unstable, but customers are in a position to minimize that instability.

Then there is Accounts Receivable. Slow paying accounts and non-paying accounts (i.e. bankruptcy filings) result in substantial costs for suppliers. This is particularly true during the economic downturn that is occurring at the time of the writing of this book. Like with all other forms of cost diversion, the supply chain responds by replenishing those losses from the customer community.

It is not easy to structure partnerships that address every eventuality, but it is not difficult for customers and suppliers to acknowledge how their independent actions can have a substantially adverse impact on mutual costs. I advocate partnerships that fully understand and openly address those costs.

Focus on Existing Relationships

One of the reasons I decided to shift my own professional focus to Lean TCO is the reality that the existing relationships customers have with their suppliers are important and potentially valuable. No matter how much I felt I could bring to the table as a new supplier for a prospective customer, I knew that any supplier… no matter how large or small… could learn to apply the methods I advocate to build powerful strategic partnerships with their customers. My personal passion is in lean methodology. I have always been more interested in the process improvements I could bring to my customers as opposed to any individual products. Even during all of my years managing new product development activity, I focused on the processes and methods that would bring successful products to the market faster, not the products themselves.

It might be more productive for your organization to build upon your existing supplier relationships than to establish new relationships. The knowledge that both you and your suppliers have based upon your history of working together has real potential value. The one-on-one relationships between your organization's personnel and your supplier's personnel are also likely to have value… if those relationships have been built primarily around supplier performance rather than golf outings and trinkets.

Speaking of golf outings, which can be fine, I will briefly digress to issues of integrity. I have not written a chapter on business ethics in part because of the exasperating experiences I have had with a lack of ethics in both buyers and sellers. The lack of ethics in the supply industry is so pervasive that if I wrote one chapter I would end up writing an entire book. So I will simply say this... if you are reading this book and suffer from a lack of business integrity, put it down and get out of my industry. If you are a reader of this book and have significant concerns about members of your organization when it comes to their relationships with suppliers, it is better to get those issues addressed first and then return to implementing the principles in this book.

Properly Align Partnership Responsibilities

Your suppliers might become concerned about their internal capabilities and service offerings as you bring them into your Lean TCO Program. They might reasonably question their organization's ability to truly help with implementing lean improvements.

We are providing the framework to produce enduring customer-supplier partnerships for mutual financial benefit, and within that context, we encourage you to ask your suppliers to take an inward look at their business methods and service offerings while taking an outward look at how those processes impact your own methods and procedures. The more they understand your organization, the better able they will be to join you in the effort to substantially reduce costs.

As you go through the Lean TCO Program with your suppliers, one of the outcomes should be clearly understood partnership responsibilities. While each of your suppliers should continue to earn the privilege of doing business with your organization, you can help the success of those partnerships by acknowledging the impact you have on costs.

The partnership can be established in a variety of forms and may or may not include a contract. I do not make any recommendations on the structure of your partnerships, only that they clearly delineate each partner's responsibilities in accordance with what is under their respective control. The customer does not package the product for shipment from the supplier, so the impact on freight cost from product packaging must be the supplier's accountability. The supplier, unless they are providing Vendor Managed Inventory (VMI) services, cannot control the size and frequency of Purchase Orders. The size and frequency of Purchase Orders is under the control of the customer, and the corresponding costs that the partnership incurs should be the responsibility of the customer. I do not recommend any financial "penalties" when one party produces an unnecessary cost to the partnership, that would be rather extreme. On the other hand, open communication about the performance of each party with respect to their responsibilities is strongly encouraged.

As you work with your suppliers to minimize costs, you should be able to align every cost category with either your organization or the supplier's. If the supplier ships 5 small boxes of supplies that have an average weight of 5 pounds, rather than one 25 pound box, the customer should speak up... even if they are not being invoiced for the freight. As in any business relationship, clearly understood and properly aligned accountabilities can mitigate costly problems and reduce unnecessary frustrations.

One major challenge that suppliers face is to reduce the risk of asset value loss. Earlier in this chapter, we briefly discussed the two primary assets to be concerned with: Inventory and Accounts Receivable.

As a supplier to a mining operation, we incurred substantial losses when they filed for bankruptcy protection following the commodity collapse of 2008. We found ourselves experiencing considerable asset devaluation... certain Accounts Receivable values going to zero and certain inventory items that had a very limited market due to the financial hit the overall US metal mining industry was experiencing. It turned out to be a very valuable lesson.

Suppliers that carry inventory and offer payment terms to customers incur risk. Those risks result in occasional losses and those losses can be substantial. Like all other supply chain costs, these losses must be covered by customers in order for any given supplier to endure. Suppliers certainly have the responsibility to manage receivables and inventory, but juggling customer expectations for terms, immediate product availability, and competitive prices is a significant challenge. How do immediate product availability and competitive prices produce risks for the supplier? Excessive inventory. When a supplier buys directly from a manufacturer, they are motivated to place large purchases in order to drive down prices paid and reduce overhead percentages. Furthermore, a lack of product availability not only can cost a supplier a sale, it can cost a supplier a customer. The result is large manufacturer-direct purchases that produce substantial inventory carrying costs and the risk of inventory asset devaluation.

Your supplier partnerships should address these inventory risks. Beyond commitments to purchase any residual inventory that a supplier might keep on hand for your facility, you should work with your suppliers with respect to how they obtain the margin they need to earn a fair profit. If your supplier quotes an item for your facility at a price that depends upon large purchases from their source, you should be aware of the corresponding risk that the partnership is taking on. It might be far more cost effective for you to accept slightly higher prices on some items in order to reduce inventory risks for the partnership. There may also be item consolidation opportunities with your supplier's sources that you can impact; consolidating some of the items your facility needs into a single manufacturer may allow your supplier to reach order minimums that produce better prices without the corresponding risk of excessive inventory in singular items.

Regarding Accounts Receivable, your suppliers must price their products and services in a manner that occasional bad receivables can be covered. Depending upon how much receivables risk they incur, their prices might be impacted substantially.

Offering terms (i.e. payment in 30 days) requires supplier capital. If you purchase an item from a supplier and pay that supplier later than the supplier must pay their source for that item, the supplier has to produce the capital to span that gap... to cover the float. As someone who always challenges the status quo due to my lean thinking, I often wondered why we as suppliers of low cost consumable items would provide banking services to customers hundreds of times our size. Why would a billion dollar corporation turn to a small distributorship and ask for an inconsequential amount of cash in the form of a short term loan? Why would a billion dollar corporation need my help in covering a $72.00 purchase?

The answer is simple, but it is not sufficient: industry buys on terms. The tiny distributor loans money to the behemoth corporation because that is the way it has always worked. If you have been through any form of lean training, you know "we have always done it this way" is never a reason for continuing to do things in that way. If the behemoth fails and files bankruptcy, restructures, and emerges from bankruptcy 2 years later, where is the tiny distributor? Long ago liquidated. If the distributor is large enough to survive customer bankruptcy filings, how are the losses covered? By you, another customer of the supplier, within prices paid. Like the car insurance discussed earlier, regardless of your driving record, you pay for other people that have accidents.

What about P-cards (procurement cards)? P-cards are another source of substantial cost within the supply chain that you must pay for. P-cards were not developed by the supply industry for immediate payment; P-cards are often used to pay suppliers in 45 to 90 days rather than at the time of shipment. They were developed as a means to reduce customer overhead expense when paying suppliers. It is much less expensive for an Accounting Department to pay one credit card bill as opposed to 100 supplier invoices. Depending upon the purchasing authority granted to P-card holders, there can also be savings associated with the elimination of Purchase Requisition approval and Purchase Order placement costs. So what's the problem with P-cards if they save on overhead expenses?

3%

The *staggering cost* to suppliers to accept payment by credit card is the problem. If you don't work for a non-profit organization, ask someone in the Finance Department what 3% in margin is worth to your organization. Ask someone in the Finance Department how they would feel about giving away 3 margin points to a third party. Ask the CEO how hard your organization works to create an extra 3 points in margin, whether through marketing or new product development efforts.

If an organization generates $500 million in annual sales, 3 margin points is $15,000,000. If that organization's profit during a tough year is 1.5%, 3 margin points turns a $7,500,000 profit into a $7,500,000 loss.

To bring the point a little closer to home, what if your employer told you that they were going to start depositing your paycheck directly into your checking account in order to avoid the cost of printing checks, and that you will see a 3% deduction in your pay as a result?

So, when your supplier is taking a 3% hit for accepting P-cards, who is paying for it? You know the answer by now.

"All supply chain costs are ultimately diverted back to the customer in prices paid."

There is an answer to this dilemma... a way to reduce your requisition, purchasing, and vendor payment overhead expenses while not requiring your customer-supplier partnerships to take a 3% hit... but there are reasons I prefer not to discuss this solution within this book. Visit www.LeanTCO.com to get in touch with us if you would like to learn what the credit card industry does not want you to know.

Suppliers: Expand Your Horizon

At the time of the writing of this book, the supply industry functions through the same fundamental processes it always has. Catalogs, even if they are now online, are looked through by customers and orders are placed with the supplier. If you are a large supplier, you may have sophisticated service offerings or retail locations that complement your catalogs, but it is likely that your printed and online catalogs remain the primary driver of your core revenue stream. It is likely that your focus is marketing supply items through whatever access methods work best for your customers.

Our premise is that TCO-based partnerships should move away from the traditional forms of conducting business, even if some of the traditional transactions between customers and suppliers remain. If we can shift buyer and seller attention away from supply items and toward supply processes, we will accomplish our goal. Our hope for you is that your interactions with customers will increasingly involve discussions of process costs and process improvements rather than supply item costs and supply item improvements.

We believe that suppliers who can make the transition from a *supply item driven business* to a *supply process driven business* will be the suppliers who dominate the supply landscape in the coming decade. Those who bring real value to customers will not be those who bring low prices but compelling methods of conducting business that minimize Total Cost of Ownership. To be sure, lower prices will result from any effective customer-supplier partnership that drives down supply chain costs... but the key phrase here is "will result from." The partnership strives to drive down costs and the partnership shares in the gains as the results of those efforts allow prices to move downward at the same time supplier profitability moves upward. We do not advocate the formation of any strategic partnership where the launch of the partnership is based on low prices.

It may be time to expand your horizons as you look at internal process costs, the process costs your customers endure, your methods of sourcing supply inventory, and the breadth of your product offerings. I can assure you that customers who are involved in a Lean TCO Program will have more confidence in their suppliers who are involved in their own internal process improvement efforts. If your internal efforts align well with your customer's internal efforts, you are miles ahead of the competition in forging that strategic partnership.

Furthermore, if you demonstrate genuine interest in the methods your customers use to manage supply inventory, you are far more likely to be invited into their organization to have a positive impact on those methods.

Chapter 7

Procurement Contracts? Proceed With Caution

Many years ago, following a corporate-level decision made by one of our customers, our supply business was fortunate to have strong working relationships in place with facility-level buyers. The buyers we served appreciated that we maintained immediate availability of the items we provided to their locations. We did not have any relationships within the corporate office, only relationships with the buyers at the individual facilities, and a corporate-level decision was made to enter into an aggressively priced purchasing contract with another supplier.

We quickly began receiving orders again since the new supplier was unable to maintain sufficient product availability. Eventually, we regained the business we had lost. Not only were the buyers disappointed that we were temporarily displaced as a supplier, they were angered by the apparent contractual protection given to the new supplier. Many of the buyers viewed the contract as protective cover for poor supplier performance.

The significance of that experience was not financial... it was not that we regained business we had lost. The significance was in what we learned from that experience.   Many consider procurement contracts as a way to protect suppliers as they stock inventory for a committed customer. The supplier can more readily assure inventory availability if they have reduced inventory risk. In this case, the procurement contract resulted in a *decrease* in the availability of supply inventory.

Procurement contracts often contain binding language that serves to drive up TCO. Contracts can be extremely difficult to draft; once signatures are required on a written document, lawyers jump in to create protective wording so that those signatures do not cause unacceptable liabilities. Liabilities associated with every aspect of a customer-supplier contract are no doubt considerable. Here is my most basic concern with procurement contracts: *partnerships should not be built around contractual liability protection.*

Fixed Pricing Might Become Fixed Losses

I had the experience of going through a deposition related to a lawsuit that had been filed by a third party against a past customer of a past business I owned. My business was not a party in the lawsuit, but the plaintiff wanted to obtain certain information about the defendant's business practices. I cannot divulge any details of that experience, but in that process I learned how written contracts can't define a business relationship no matter how lengthy or well-worded. It is simply impossible for written contracts to define every potential eventuality that can occur in a business relationship. Lawyers can make a great deal of money trying to cover every detail, and the harder they try, the more money they make. And yes, any legal expenses associated with supply item procurement must be considered a component of TCO.

Procurement contracts can contain such binding legal jargon that they serve to damage the business relationship between the parties they are trying to protect. I will take one simple example to emphasize this point. Many procurement contracts seek to establish fixed pricing over a specified period of time. In my opinion, fixed pricing can make sense for raw materials purchased by a manufacturing organization where those raw materials represent a substantial percentage of their total operating budget. The ability to negotiate fixed pricing may help a manufacturer assure that operating margins will be acceptable over the term of the contract with the supplier. For supply items, though, fluctuations in purchase prices should not substantially impact an organization's Profit and Loss statement.   There can be periods of time where prices can move downward, even dramatically, as they did across many commodities in late 2008 and early 2009.   Fixed pricing contracts prevent customers from achieving savings when prices drop.

What about when prices rise?   I argue that fixed pricing contracts where the supplier's margins become unacceptably low do not reflect strategic partnerships.   Most   procurement   professionals   desire mutually beneficial relationships with suppliers that can endure, and they generally desire working with financially stable organizations. Fixed pricing contracts have a purpose: to benefit the customer at the potential expense of the supplier.   This is a form of cost diversion rather than cost control, and you know by now my position on how damaging cost diversion can be to strategic partnerships and their mutual costs.

If you are a buyer that advocates fixed pricing, you might express three legitimate arguments for fixed pricing contracts.   First, they may eliminate the need for review and approval of pricing adjustments throughout the term of the contract.   In some organizations, blanket Purchase   Orders   are   used   to   reduce   expenses   associated   with processing individual Purchase Orders.   Those blanket orders are often awarded to suppliers based upon a fixed price quote for a specified term.   Second, the supplier benefits from knowing that the inventory they are carrying for fixed price items is going to be consumed (no risk of dead inventory). Third, your supplier can confidently purchase more inventory of an item with more purchasing power.

Here is my challenge for those three arguments. To the first point, you should question the idea that PO's issued to a strategic partner for standardized supply items should go through an approval process. If management knows that efficient and accurate inventory control methods are in place for standardized items... purchased by procurement professionals from strategic partners... they are far less likely to require formal PO approvals. To the second point, strategic partners should not be left with dead inventory regardless of contracts, unless the supplier made supply procurement decisions that were not to the benefit of the partnership. To the third point, if the strategic partnership is addressing all mutual costs, the issue of supplier purchase volume will be discussed and addressed. Again, accurate inventory control methods for standardized items is the key. Suppliers will know usage patterns for standard items and can manage their safety stock accordingly. Within the strategic partnership, customers should be happy to consume that safety stock if they decide to make a change to another item, particularly since that safety stock should never be excessive.

Strategic partnerships aside, there is a far more important reason to avoid fixed pricing contracts. In my supply business, I had one customer that required fixed pricing agreements in order for my company to be selected as a source for blanket PO's. I would generally avoid these types of purchasing agreements. In the defense of the buyer at this account, a very capable procurement professional that was highly structured in her approach to her work, she was solely responsible for all consumable supplies used at a facility that had substantial spend on indirect materials along with considerable inventory control challenges. The controls she had implemented within her own area of responsibility allowed her to handle a tremendous workload. Blanket PO's were a form of that control.

For a supplier, fixed pricing agreements are a tremendous challenge. You want to offer a price that the buyer will recognize as competitive, but you can't afford the risk of your margins collapsing, or worse, becoming negative, if your cost for the item rises during the term of the agreement. During the commodity boom in that ended in 2008, we had prices from some manufacturers nearly double. Had any of those products been under fixed pricing agreements, I would have been shipping those products at a tremendous loss. So responsible suppliers have only one choice when quoting fixed price agreements... to quote higher prices to offset the risk of future losses.

I suggest that customers and suppliers leave the gambling to Las Vegas and the financial markets; it has no place in healthy strategic partnerships. If management is concerned about potential price increases, tell them that there are plenty of hedge funds in the financial markets where they can place their bets.

Performance-Based Partnerships

With or without contracts, all effective customer-supplier partnerships need to be based upon performance. As a partnership, both sides must perform to retain the benefit of doing business with the other party. Let me say it again this way... although the supplier needs to continuously earn the business of the customer, the customer also has an obligation to perform in the best interest of the partnership. Outstanding suppliers that form high-value strategic partnerships with their customers are likely to have greater expectations of their customers than suppliers that are looking to land any sale they can.

By definition, contracts afford protection. They are intended to control the conduct of the parties who sign. Thus, by definition, they can hinder partnerships. On the other hand, contracts can serve to provide an explicit understanding of a partnership agreement, assuring that both parties have a full understanding of their rights and obligations under the contract. Contracts can also allow both parties to make commitments that may otherwise expose them to excessive risk. Contracts can allow parties to move forward with confidence.

If you decide to enter into a contractual arrangement with a supplier, I encourage you to generate that contract together. I do not recommend that a contract from a supplier be signed by a customer, nor do I recommend that a contract from a customer be signed by a supplier. I am not a lawyer so I cannot offer any legal advice on specific contract content. Get the spirit of the partnership hammered out in layman's terms, and then allow the legal professionals to create the proper embodiment of the agreement.

Chapter 8

Measure, Analyze, and Improve TCO Performance

A word of caution, and opportunity, to Six Sigma experts. I have written this chapter without including the analytical tools of Six Sigma. Recognize that this book is written in a manner that readers without a Six Sigma background are able to launch and execute a successful Lean TCO Program. If you have in-depth Six Sigma experience, I encourage you to apply that experience to the overall approach defined in this chapter.

The Relentless Elimination of Waste

I was fortunate to start my career in the early 1980's with a company that was embracing Just-In-Time (JIT) methods. A major manufacturer of telecommunications equipment, they had sales of less than $100 million when I joined the company and ultimately became a multi-billion dollar manufacturer many years after I left. I believe their success resulted from their demand for excellence in every facet of the corporation.

JIT could be described as the original lean initiative. Like all initiatives that gain popularity in the manufacturing sector, they are met with varying degrees of success within the corporations that deploy them. My first employer was highly successful with JIT; that success had a significant impact on my own career. I am a firm believer in the phrase that defined JIT as "The Relentless Elimination of Waste" and I have applied that phrase with rigor in every position I have held and now as a business owner. *The relentless elimination of waste is at the core of everything written in this book.* If you get nothing more from this chapter, remember that it is aggressively searching for and destroying waste that produces highly efficient and highly effective processes that maximize performance and minimize cost.

A variety of lean initiatives have come and gone over the years, but if there is one that will stand the test of time, it will be Six Sigma.

During the early days of my career, Six Sigma was a quality initiative rather than the broad-sweeping lean initiative it is today. Six Sigma involved production process optimization that reduced product defects. The primary pursuit behind Six Sigma was the reduction of process variance since process variance is the primary cause of defects. Six Sigma applied statistical tools to the measurement, reduction, and control of process variance.

Today, Six Sigma is better known as an initiative that applies many tools (including some statistical tools) to improve process efficiency. Organizations that have implemented formal Six Sigma programs can make substantial investments in employee training and often dedicate personnel to the full time application of Six Sigma methods. I will cover a few of the key elements of Six Sigma that can be effectively applied to our TCO reduction efforts.

In my opinion, the first and most important distinction of a Six Sigma lean initiative is the top-down structure of how projects get approved and launched. Six Sigma requires the head of the organization to be directly involved in which projects get launched and which projects don't. The top-level management team has project reporting responsibility, and typically, the project leaders report to the management team. This top-down responsibility not only assures that the most important projects get approved and implemented, it also provides clear communication to the entire organization that Six Sigma projects are a major corporate priority.

If your organization has a Six Sigma program in place, I strongly urge that the Lean TCO Program be reviewed and approved by management as a formal Six Sigma project… it will help to assure that the project is given a high level of visibility and will benefit from greater internal support.

The Lean TCO Triangle

Too many organizations fail to consider the complex interdependencies between items, suppliers, and internal processes when making sourcing decisions or pursuing cost reduction efforts. For example, the selection of an otherwise ideal supply item might be a poor choice if a new supplier must be set up in order to obtain that item. The relationships between items, suppliers, and processes must be fully understood and accounted for throughout your Lean TCO Program; effective decisions in one area cannot be made without understanding the impact of those decisions in the other two areas. The Lean TCO Triangle below is a visual reference to remind your Lean TCO Program team to take an integrated approach in their improvement efforts.

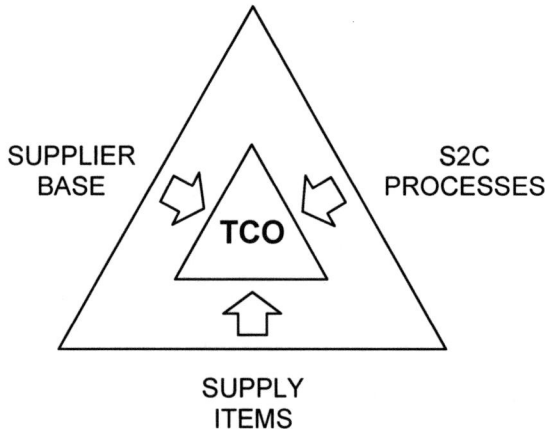

While the Lean TCO Triangle emphasizes the breadth and complexity of your Lean TCO Program, it can also be used to describe how costs can spiral upward over time if controls are not put in place. Just as more items can lead to more suppliers, more suppliers... through greater product selection options for employees... can lead to more items. More items and more suppliers then leads to more process execution time to obtain, store, distribute, and pay for supply inventory. When process execution challenges fail to meet the supply needs of employees, the purchase of new items can result... so the cycle continues. The Lean TCO Triangle provides insight as to why organizations can struggle to get control: the complexity of the relationships between items, suppliers, and processes can cause even the most experienced cost reduction experts to back away.

It is appropriate to point out here why I do not provide a singular solution to the challenge of minimizing TCO. The path to minimizing TCO requires hard internal work and true partnering with your suppliers. Your item needs are unique, your organizational structure is unique, your supply related processes are unique, and the relationships between your suppliers and your personnel are unique. It is not feasible to tear all of that down and replace it with a one-fits-all solution. If that was possible, the supply industry would have already given you that solution and you would not be reading this book.

I will also again comment here that the substantial challenge of reducing TCO is too often met with sudden decisions to turn control over to a Vendor Managed Inventory solution or to a Business Process

Outsourcing service provider (see Chapter 4). They are viable options, but at this stage, they are nothing more than that. I encourage organizations to use the tools and techniques in this book to first establish control and drive down costs. At that point, better cost comparisons between internal solutions and external service options can be made. Furthermore, any handoff to external services can occur under controlled circumstances with dramatically reduced risks.

What's in a Measurement?

The ability to present information in the form of numbers allows that information to be more readily processed and acted upon. There is a big difference between saying "We are slow at receiving product" than saying "On average, confirming a packing list against a supply shipment takes 14.7 minutes." Measurement will allow your Lean TCO Program team to understand the costs associated with your current items, processes, and suppliers.

Measurement will also involve mapping out your current processes to establish a clear understanding of how employees carry out all activities associated with supply items. Process mapping produces flow charts of those activities. It is important to understand how all of your processes are interconnected before beginning the detailed process mapping activity shown a little later in this chapter.

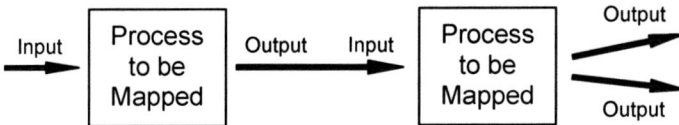

Input → | Process to be Mapped | → Output Input → | Process to be Mapped | → Output / Output

Inputs and outputs can have many forms... including forms themselves. If an employee fills out a Purchase Requisition form that must be approved prior to issuing a Purchase Order, that form will be an input to a Purchase Requisition Approval process. The output would be the approval status of the requisition, and if approved, the requisition would become the input to the Purchase Order process.

In a Six Sigma program, the primary objective of the Measure phase is to determine the relatively few factors that have the most significant impact on your processes. More specifically, Six Sigma is looking to measure process performance with respect to the key factors that cause process variance. Think in terms of excessive process variance resulting in excessive cost. Due to the breadth of your Lean TCO Program, you will be looking at a large number of interrelated processes during the Measure phase and you will be trying to determine the relatively few factors that impact each of those processes. You will find that there are common factors that affect multiple processes, and the effectiveness of your measurements related to those factors will have a substantial affect on the overall success of your program.

As you can imagine, a common factor in many supply related processes that has a direct correlation to costs is the number of unique items in use. A reduction in the number of unique items will have a direct impact on costs across many processes. Another common factor will be the size of purchases. Generally speaking, as a percentage of prices paid, purchasing, receiving, and vendor payment process costs decrease as order sizes increase. At the completion of the Measure phase, the Lean TCO Program team will have a clear understanding of all supply related processes and all corresponding costs.

If you are a buyer, ask yourself what is the most commonly used seller approach to try and win your business. If you are a seller, ask yourself what is the most common reason your prospect won't change sources. If I took a poll of all buyers and sellers, I expect that "price" would be at the top of the list of answers. I expect that "free freight" or "free delivery" would be second on the list.

It is likely that many readers have been involved in a few sales discussions represented by the following exchange:

> **Seller:** "We sell value. It is our service that distinguishes us from the competition."
>
> **Prospect:** "Good, I don't make sourcing decisions based on price. Tell me about your services."
>
> **Seller:** "We will work closely with your employees to make sure they are getting what they need when they need it. We will keep inventory in stock just for you and we will ship same-day for orders received by 2:00 pm."
>
> **Prospect:** "Great. I'll put together a list of items that you can quote."

What is the last document most sellers prepare before landing a new account? What is the last document most buyers look at before giving a new supplier an order? The quote.

The point here is this. We all gravitate toward what is easily measured. Our purchasing decisions as consumers are based largely on considerations that can be broken down into numbers. Price, ounces, calories, pixels, megabytes, gas mileage, and so on. Our consumer buying decisions that are not made solely on numbers must first meet our numerical requirements. Affordability... size... specifications... even the purchase of a home that involves so many un-measurable considerations must meet certain measurable requirements. Price, number of bedrooms, square feet, and distance from work are just a few that can knock the otherwise ideal home off of the list.

When it comes to Lean TCO, the unfortunate reality is that the hard-to-measure costs are the most important. Consider the following list of example TCO cost drivers. How would you rank these in terms of measurement difficulty (1 = easiest to measure, 8 = hardest to measure)?

___ Prices Paid

___ Freight

___ Overhead Costs

___ Shrinkage

___ Item Quality Issues

___ Item Suitability Issues

___ Downtime due to Stock Outs

How would you rank these same cost drivers in terms of impact (1 = most costly, 8 = least costly)?

___ Prices Paid

___ Freight

___ Overhead Costs

___ Shrinkage

___ Item Quality Issues

___ Item Suitability Issues

___ Downtime due to Stock Outs

Sourcing decisions drift towards the most easily measured components of cost. Most readers will rank prices paid and freight as relatively easy to measure. The other cost categories are much more difficult to assess. Ironically, when we make these other categories the focus of our cost reduction efforts and resist the temptation to focus on prices, prices should naturally come down.

From a Six Sigma perspective, measuring processes can only occur with respect to the desired outcomes of those processes. What is the desired outcome of a receiving process? If you answered "product that has been properly received" you have answered accurately... but not completely with respect to Six Sigma. What other outcome might be desirable? Beyond accuracy, you will be interested in the efficiency of the process. You will be seeking the critical factors that impact both accuracy and efficiency and then working to impact those factors.

In order for your Lean TCO Program team to measure the total TCO reduction they achieve, it is necessary to know how much is being spent currently in terms of prices paid. Do not seek out individual supply item prices but overall spend within supply item categories. Discrete price savings on individual items might be of some interest, but the overall reduction in prices paid is not likely to correlate well with data gathered from individual items. This is due to the fact that an effective Lean TCO Program will impact the items your organization uses; some items will be consolidated and others changed.

It is important to select a broad enough timeframe that the total spend information you obtain will have greater statistical significance. I recommend gathering data for the 12 months prior to the launch of your Lean TCO Program. It is also important to consider the business conditions during that span of time. Sales volumes, product mix, special projects, and other factors could have influenced indirect material spend in ways that the team should account for. As a simple example, the team could divide spend by revenue for the prior 12 month period and then scale future spend information in the same way. If your organization's sales were up by 10% during a period of time that a 20% reduction in supply item spend occurred, that is a more substantial team performance than if sales were down by 10% during that same period.

Process Mapping

You will not be able to simply send your Lean TCO Program team members out into your facility with stopwatches and calculators and expect them to return with good data. It is necessary to establish an overall approach to your measurement activity and then provide your team with the appropriate measurement tools. This begins with process mapping.

Process mapping is the creation of a graphical representation of workflow. Effective process mapping requires the breakdown of a large and complex process, such as getting a supply item from a supplier to an employee, into a more manageable subset of processes. Your Lean TCO Program is likely to involve dozens of discrete process maps that are all interconnected.

The degree of process breakdown should be related to the degree of process complexity. As a rule of thumb, if a process cannot be described in fewer than 50 steps, break that process down into sub-processes. Start with a division of supply items into individual supply categories. Examples might include the following:

Maintenance Consumables
Maintenance and Repair Parts
Industrial Supplies
Safety Supplies

First Aid Supplies

Office Supplies

Janitorial Products

Look at your supply related processes for each supply category. I recommend the following:

Selection: How supply items are selected and approved for use.

Requisition: The process employees follow to request the purchase of a supply item.

Procurement: The various methods used to obtain supply items.

Receiving: The process of confirming a supplier shipment against a packing list.

Stocking: The movement of received supply items to supply storage areas.

Distribution: The methods used to get supply items to employees.

Vendor Payment: The accounting processes used to pay vendors.

Return to your list of supply categories. If substantially different processes are used within some of the categories, consider breaking those down into separate categories that follow consistent processes. For example, if you have a Maintenance Department that uses a Vendor Managed Inventory (VMI) solution for fasteners only, you should create a separate Maintenance Fasteners category.

In my opinion, "sticky notes" are the most effective process mapping tool. Consider the complex process of heating soup in the microwave (my wife would tell you that I find any cooking process to be a challenge). To map this process, bring the appropriate team members into the conference room and discuss the process. Break down the process into key steps that can be readily analyzed. Put those key steps on sticky notes and place them on the conference room wall in the sequence they are performed:

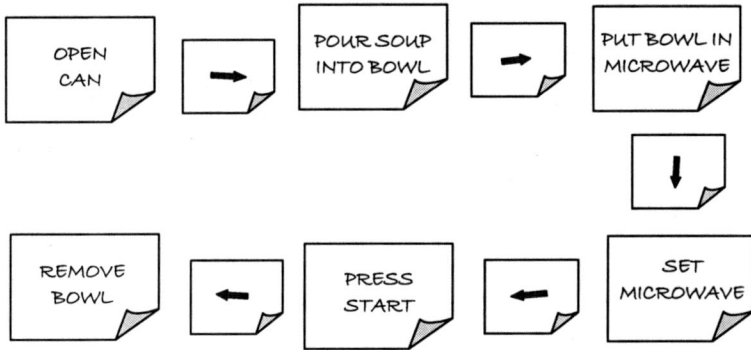

Some team members may voice their opinions about how the soup heating process should be performed in the future. Gently remind them that they need to remain focused on the current soup heating process and that they will have plenty of opportunity to rearrange the sticky notes into a recommended new process at a later date.

Let's say that the team studies the process and decides that they need to get some clarification. They're not sure whether or not a can opener is needed. The team assigns an action item to one of the team members to get the necessary information. The team reconvenes and considers the new input: the can opener is sometimes required, but some soup cans have a pull-off top. To make things more complex, the team member reports that some of the soup cans are actually bowls themselves. More sticky notes are created and moved around on the conference room wall until the team agrees that the process map reflects current practice.

Your process maps will need to be created with a logical level of detail. If you were in the business of preparing soup for hundreds of customers at a time, the level of detail in this example might be appropriate... particularly since you might go out of business heating soup in a microwave one serving at a time.

If you were analyzing the receiving process, you would not start the process with "obtain a box cutter." It would be more appropriate to start that process with a step to confirm the incoming shipment against the packing list. (By the way, if your measurement activity actually determined that receiving personnel were spending time searching for box cutters, you would get that addressed with 5S as discussed in Chapter 2.)

After completing a sticky note process map, software can be used to create a process flow chart. The flow chart is now ready and waiting for measurement work as the team members turn their attention to the next process. We recommend that all process flowcharts follow this naming convention: "Flow Chart xxy", where xx is a sequentially assigned number and y is a revision letter. We also recommend the use of a supporting word processing document named "Process Notes xxy" for organizing all other process information the team generates. (Visit www.LeanTCO.com to download free copies of forms for flow charts and process notes. You will need to register if you have not already done so.) A process-specific word processing document is a great place to capture a variety of information, including process owners, responsible team members, key findings, process improvement ideas, related suppliers, and related supply items. The structure of the document is not critical; just capture the information the team will use throughout the project. The structure of each document should be consistent and I recommend the use of Measure, Analyze, Improve, and Control sections. I also recommend a "Related Files" section for any other documents the team would like to attach to the process.

Seeking the Root Cause of Process Variance

From a Six Sigma perspective, process variance is what can cause unacceptable process output. This can be easy to understand from a manufacturing viewpoint where a product must conform to specifications. If the length of a manufactured part must be within a tolerance range, such as 2.000 inches long +/- .010 inches, a production process that produces parts that are 2.011 long or longer is producing unacceptable output. It can be a little harder to grasp process variance when it is applied to process output that cannot be measured as readily as the length of a production part.

Your Lean TCO Program should create what I call Selection to Consumption (S2C) processes that are stable and repeatable; processes that do not produce variance that drives up Total Cost of Ownership. There will be some processes your team analyzes where the measurements will be relatively easy. Any process that involves a measurable amount of time will allow your team to focus on reducing the corresponding manpower costs. Process variance may reveal time expenditures that can be minimized or eliminated. For example, when your team is analyzing the vendor payment process, backorders could be revealed as a root cause of process variance that increases the amount of time expended to issue a check. The number of backorders experienced with your current suppliers could then become a targeted improvement area.

Variance in other processes will be more challenging to analyze. You will be addressing your supply item selection process early in your Lean TCO Program. It is difficult to establish process variance measurements related to how your employees select a supply item for use, but as you have read previously, the lack of a consistent and controlled method for introducing new supply items is a primary cause of excessive TCO. If you have 5 unique supply items that all address the same need, the "variance" in the selection process is the selection process output of 5 supply items as opposed to a single supply item. The potential TCO impact is overhead expense that is 5 times what it would otherwise be if there was no variance in the supply selection process.

How to Overcome Resistance and Standardize

Before getting into your S2C processes, I need to address the issue of item standardization in some detail. The Lean TCO Program team needs to be prepared to face some resistance as they attempt to gain control of how supply items will be selected for use.

I believe standardization should occur in all aspects of product and process design. Standardization makes efficiency possible. Imagine a world without standard household outlets… supplying power to a table lamp would no longer be a 3 second task. Consider the challenge of getting from your home to the office if there was no common understanding that you drive on the right side of the road.

For a variety of reasons, industry generally fails to effectively standardize on supply items. The single greatest barrier to standardization is personal preference. Without controls in place, employees will attempt to obtain the supply items that meet their own preferences. The look and feel of a glove or the brand name of a tool are examples of primary drivers in supply item selection. Closely related is the preference of certain suppliers based upon personal relationships.

Many corporations make the mistake of attempting corporate mandates to get supply item costs back under control. These efforts often fail due to the frustrations that supply item users can experience.

Like any worthwhile process improvement effort, standardization must be executed with a thorough assessment that involves those who are affected by potential changes. I recommend the following approach:

1. Announce the standardization effort well in advance of selecting standard items.

2. Appoint responsible individuals by commodity category. Use these individuals to gather information from affected employees and make recommendations.

3. Communicate the connection between standardization and profit performance. This is particularly important if your company has a profit sharing program.

4. Consider all feedback. Not only will this improve the likelihood that the best items are selected, there will be far more support if supply item users know they had the chance to be heard. Don't underestimate the attachment workers may have to the items they use, and don't underestimate the value of their input.

5. Involve your suppliers. Let them know that you will need their help in evaluating alternatives. Obtain free samples as appropriate.

6. Distinguish branding and marketing from value. Although well branded and well marketed products can be the best alternative, it is likely that less costly items can be just as effective at getting the job done.

7. Allow users to recommend items and to place items under formal evaluation as appropriate.

It is important to remember that items are not only procured and managed through processes, but that they are used within processes themselves. It is easy to overlook the critical area of how well items perform with respect to their assigned task. A low grade abrasive product may have an attractive price when compared to a high grade abrasive product, but if the higher grade abrasive will outlast the lower grade alternative, it may be less expensive from a TCO perspective. A product with three times the endurance at twice the price is likely to offer more value.

Manufacturers may offer multiple grades of the same product, and similar products may be available from multiple manufacturers. A broad variety of choices can make an evaluation of alternatives very challenging. I offer the following guidelines:

1. Worker safety comes first.

2. Regulatory compliance, where applicable, is mandatory.

3. Perform evaluations by testing product alternatives in their applications by the employees who use them.

4. Measure alternatives in item cost per unit of time (i.e. $1.24/hour).

5. Account for potential product loss (work gloves used off-site may only need to last one day if they are not likely to be brought back by the worker the following day).

6. The relative value of items that must be sourced through a new supplier might be offset by the cost of doing business with that supplier.

7. Selecting items from suppliers with narrow product availability may limit future supplier consolidation.

8. The relative value of items that require any unique S2C (Selection to Consumption) processes might be offset by process costs.

Consistent with the Lean TCO Triangle, all *items* selected based upon performance within their application must not incur offsetting expenses with respect to *suppliers* and *processes*.

Material Safety Data Sheets

Material Safety Data Sheet (MSDS) management is an often-overlooked area of potential cost savings associated with consumable supplies. The Occupational Safety and Health Administration (OSHA) requires employers to have an MSDS available for each product that poses a potential hazard to employees. Compliance to OSHA requirements for MSDS management can be costly and should be reviewed within your Lean TCO Program.

Employers must demonstrate that they know what hazards their employees are exposed to, that their employees have been made aware of those hazards, and that appropriate protective measures have been implemented. They must assure that an MSDS for any given product currently in use is readily accessible and that MSDS archiving requirements are met. Employers must remain up-to-date on corresponding OSHA requirements at all times since those requirements can change.

Many organizations use notebooks for MSDS management. Assuring compliance using exclusively paper-based methods is extremely costly, particularly when the risk of lost Material Safety Data Sheets is properly accounted for. (An employee might remove an MSDS from a notebook, resulting in non-compliance and the need to replace that MSDS immediately... frequent audits of notebooks is necessary to assure they remain in compliance.) Any change in an MSDS requires manual updates of all affected notebooks. When a new MSDS is added to a notebook, the indexing documents used to locate an MSDS within each notebook must also be updated.

Regulatory compliance also applies to the Environmental Protection Agency (EPA). Depending upon on-site quantities and usage levels of chemicals that are potentially hazardous to the environment, and in the event of chemical spills, the chemical composition data (CAS data) contained in the MSDS determines what actions must be taken by the employer.

A variety of MSDS management software and services are available to help reduce costs. I recommend the use of an online MSDS management system that is supplemented by notebooks. Visit www.LeanTCO.com to learn about our online MSDS Access solution.

Chapter 9

Selection to Consumption (S2C) Processes

Many organizations look at the Procure to Pay (P2P) cycle when implementing improvement programs. Logically, it appears on the surface that supply-related processes begin with procurement and conclude with vendor payment. As you read previously, I have defined the S2C acronym as *Selection* to *Consumption* processes since Total Cost of Ownership is impacted by activities that both precede and follow the P2P cycle. In this chapter, I provide some overall guidance for your improvement efforts by looking at S2C processes in greater detail.

Selection and Sourcing

Consider the various ways supply items are specified in your organization. Who has the authority to specify an item in each supply category? How do employees know what supply items are currently available at your facility? Are your sourcing options controlled in order to prevent an expanding supplier base? If so, how do employees know which sources are approved? How do they access product information from those sources?

Selecting items to purchase not only involves the cost of the time spent in the selection process, but also results in critical TCO outcomes based upon the suitability of those items. If supply item selection occurs in your organization through random processes rather than controlled processes, how will your organization know that any given supply item has the best balance between cost and performance?

Once a supply item is selected, it must be sourced. If an item is selected by an employee from a supply catalog, the source would be the provider of the catalog. If an employee responds to an advertisement for an item, the source would be the advertiser or one of the advertiser's distributors. If a new piece of equipment is purchased that has consumable components (such as ink cartridges for a printer), the source of the components would be the manufacturer or one of the manufacturer's distributors. There is risk that an organization's supplier base could become substantially larger than necessary if supply item sourcing decisions occur outside of documented processes.

If the Purchasing Department is involved in selecting a source, the time spent in identifying that source is another component of TCO. As with item selection, a lack of controlled processes for selecting sources has significant TCO ramifications.

We will first look at the interdependencies between items and suppliers. On the surface, you may believe that the only real consideration here is which suppliers offer which items... choose an item not available from a current supplier and you will need a new supplier. In reality, the interdependency between items and suppliers is far more complex when it comes to minimizing TCO.

Consider the supplier's own product sourcing methods. Suppliers, like their customers, need to source a variety of items from a variety of sources. Some of those sources represent strategic relationships where other sources exist only to provide a well rounded product offering. Some purchases are made directly with manufacturers where others may be made through wholesale distributors. Some items are in stock and others are obtained by their source only after receiving a customer order. Suppliers will often reach cost-reducing order minimums with some of their sources while they will not with others. Suppliers, like their customers, experience varying levels of on-time delivery performance with their sources. When accounting for these various factors, the existence of an item in a supplier's catalog does not necessarily indicate that the supplier is a good candidate for sourcing that item.

The number one priority of any effective Lean TCO Program is the dependable availability of supply items for your organization's employees. This is due to the fact that the number one driver of TCO is stock outs; a needed item that is not available to an employee can represent dramatic expense compared to all other TCO cost drivers. Even if there is no work stoppage associated with a stock out, substantial expense will occur in getting the stock out addressed. Your supplier doesn't just need to have the item available, they must have the item readily available in accordance with your supply control methods. A special order item that has a 3 week lead-time, no matter how low the price, is not sourced properly if your supply control methods depend upon that item having a 3 day lead-time.

If the lead-time consideration has been satisfactorily addressed, the next primary consideration is the breadth of products currently or potentially purchased from that supplier. If the supplier currently sources 3 low-cost items and there is no reason to anticipate a measurable increase in business volume in the future, it may be better to source those items from another supplier that has a more substantial business relationship with your organization.

If the breadth of product offering consideration has been satisfactorily addressed, and if item and process interdependencies have been satisfactorily addressed as discussed later in this chapter, purchase prices can be considered.

Notice that purchase prices are considered last, not first. Product availability and breadth of product offering are not only more important than price from a TCO perspective, product breadth gives the customer-supplier partnership a better opportunity to drive down supply chain costs. This, in turn, can lead to future price reductions that still allow the supplier to earn a fair profit.

As a word of caution, do not select items that are only available from one or a limited number of suppliers unless absolutely necessary. If you select items that substantially narrow your potential sources of supply, you will also narrow your future sourcing options. Furthermore, items that have limited distribution channels are often more expensive than competitive alternatives. Manufacturers can choose to limit distribution channels based upon relationships they have with distributors as well as the desire to limit competitive quotation activity on their products.

As a distributor, I had been involved in a large quote opportunity where the prospective customer was seeking to consolidate suppliers. A protective garment was included in the items to be quoted. We contacted the manufacturer of the garment to obtain pricing in order to respond to the quote opportunity. The manufacturer indicated that they were working through a single distributor and that we would not be able to quote the product. This not only limited our ability to provide comprehensive sourcing to the prospect, it limited the prospect to only one source for that item. Although this was a frustration for us as a supplier, it was a significant liability for the customer when they launched their supplier consolidation effort.

Item selection also needs to account for how that item will be requisitioned, purchased, received, stocked, and distributed. As your Lean TCO Program progresses, internal process improvements will become a central part of TCO reduction efforts. Items selected for use must be consistent with those internal processes.

Employees might use earplugs for hearing protection and obtain those earplugs from dispensers. If a new earplug is selected that cannot be placed in the dispensers, the process of how earplugs are distributed to employees will have to change. If an item is being selected that has shelf life or warranty considerations, the process that assures First-In-First-Out (FIFO) use of the item might be affected. A new item that replaces an existing Vendor Managed Inventory item will affect requisition, purchasing, and stocking processes.

The interdependencies between suppliers and processes are almost as complex as the interdependencies between suppliers and items. As discussed in Chapter 4, there are a large number of sourcing options when it comes to consumable supplies. As these options are considered within your Lean TCO Program, the corresponding processes must be contrasted with supplier capabilities and supplier performance. The capabilities and performance of selected suppliers can substantially impact S2C processes.

Consider again the various ways your organization currently specifies supply items. For some items, the process might be very informal, such as an employee selecting an item from a catalog and contacting the Purchasing department. In other cases, the process might be much more rigorous, such as a head-to-head evaluation of alternative items to make certain the item specified is the best suited for the application. In what ways do your current suppliers impact those decisions? Is it merely through printed or on-line catalogs?

As I stated previously, item specification and standardization is the foundation of your Lean TCO Program. It would make sense, then, that the ability of your suppliers to assist in that process is critical to your overall success. Here are a number of considerations:

1. How does the supplier provide you with the information needed to make good item selection decisions?

2. Do they have sufficient knowledge and experience to gather the information you need?

3. Do they have a broad product offering that allows you to select from a variety of alternatives?

4. Can they connect you with manufacturers when appropriate in order to facilitate technical support?

Recognize that the size of the supplier is not an essential consideration in this area. Most manufacturers, whether working directly or through manufacturer representatives, provide excellent support to small distributors. When it comes to supporting product selection, what is most critical is the responsiveness and the resourcefulness of your supplier.

Requisition

An effective supply item requisition process is essential to minimizing Total Cost of Ownership and should address the following key considerations:

- Your Supply Item Master List must be readily available to your employees in order to avoid unnecessary requisitions for new items.

- An efficient method to obtain new items must be in place such that lead times for obtaining new items do not result in costly work delays.

- Sourcing methods must be in place to assure approved suppliers are used whenever possible to avoid unnecessary expansion of your supplier base.

- Review and approval mechanisms must be in place to assure that any new items and sources are consistent with Lean TCO objectives.

Random and uncontrolled requests to your Purchasing Department for new supply items must not be supported if the success of your Lean TCO Program is going to be sustained. At the same time, it is essential that your Purchase Requisition process be highly efficient so that urgently needed new items can be sourced and obtained quickly.

Your internal processes for handling requisitions can be substantially impacted by your supplier base. Routine requisitions for standard items are not likely to involve your suppliers until Purchase Orders are placed, but requisitions for new or non-standard items can involve your suppliers well before a Purchase Order is issued. Like the previous discussion on item selection, you need to assess the responsiveness of your suppliers when it comes to the inevitable requests for items that have not been purchased previously.

These requests are often urgent. Even within the well-structured systems you will have in place after you have completed your Lean TCO Program, employees will occasionally have urgent needs for something new. My experience in the supply business has taught me how important responsiveness is when buyers need support in selecting a new item. The most urgent calls typically offer little detail. "I need something we can use to handle sharp objects" might be all the information we get as we jump into sourcing a new work glove. We would work with the buyer to learn more about the nature of the "sharp objects" and the nature of the corresponding work activity. We would then offer manufacturer information on a variety of options from our own standard sources.

In some cases, buyers with urgent needs place calls to suppliers and have to leave a voicemail. If you are a supplier, let me assure you that it does not help to tell your customer in your voicemail message that you are "assisting other customers or away from your desk." You might as well say "I really don't feel like answering my phone right now" because your customer has no interest in why you can't take a call. Your message needs to indicate how the caller can get in touch with someone immediately if the need is urgent. If the buyer has to hang up the phone without speaking with someone that can assure action is taken on an urgent request, I argue that you cannot consistently perform at a level that the buyer must be able to depend upon.

The same concept applies to email. As a seller, if you are not immediately responsive to urgent emails, the buyer may need to make other sourcing decisions. If you are a buyer, you know how frustrating it is to leave messages and emails with 3 or 4 different parties within a supplier's organization and wonder if you are going to fail your internal customer in addressing their need. Even if the internal customer is at fault for a lack of planning, no buyer wants to have a non-responsive supplier be partly to blame for a the inability to quickly obtain an urgently needed item.

Unanswered phones and emails can dramatically increase the time it takes to get a sudden need addressed. It is common that the buyer does not have a manufacturer, let alone a part number, in mind when they call. There may be 10 to 20 phone calls and emails circulating in a flurry between the buyer, the internal customer, the supplier, and the supplier's sources all in the attempt to respond to the request. Add 1 hour of delay between each communication effort and what should happen in 20 minutes may take 3 days.

For whatever reason, my experience has been that the urgent requests rarely involve products that are going to be purchased by the customer in any volume. In other words, responding to urgent requests is costly and it rarely leads to measurable business in those urgently needed items. At the same time, being responsive to urgent requests for small purchases is to take advantage of the opportunity to demonstrate to your customers just how much they are appreciated. Spend 2 hours addressing an urgently needed $23 purchase, impress the customer in the process, and you've gained better marketing than any New York City advertising firm could offer.

Procurement Methods

As you already know, there are a broad variety of methods that customers and suppliers use to place and receive orders. Phone, email, online catalog, facsimile, and even walk-in orders at retail locations are common. Let me digress on that last one for a moment.

Sending an employee to a retailer to obtain supply items may not be a part of your standard ordering methods, but if you are like most organizations, it can happen far too frequently. Costs and liability risks associated with a trip to a retailer are extreme. Not only is it important that you not depend upon trips to retailers for any supplies, it is essential that you implement sufficient supply controls so that an employee never has to head out to a retailer for something they need.

Getting back to your standard order placement methods, to reduce your order processing costs, it is important to work with your suppliers in standardizing your internal processes. How orders are placed, how order acknowledgements are received, and how order acknowledgements are handled (including price changes, backorders, freight charges, and other issues) all represent process costs and should be streamlined. Establishing common processes across your supplier base, as much as practical, is a key to driving those process costs down.

More than just the various ways your supplier base can receive and acknowledge orders, it is necessary to consider any on-site services your suppliers may provide and how those services impact purchasing activity. Depending on the nature of the services (equipment inspections, janitorial services, etc.), there may be a reasonable level of dependence upon certain suppliers.

I advocate the use of electronic ordering methods whenever possible to reduce customer order placement and supplier order processing costs. Manual faxing of Purchase Orders should be avoided completely. Even automated facsimile and emailed Purchase Orders can be expensive depending upon how those orders are created. Electronic Data Interchange (EDI) systems can be efficient if they are not driven by supply inventory transactions and if they do not require extensive IT support. Visit www.LeanTCO.com to learn how our Supply Control Systems online software can support rapid creation of Purchase Orders across all of your suppliers using data from Visual Supply Management methods.

Vendor Managed Inventory (VMI) can be the most expensive way to generate order requirements. Remember that we are looking at customer-supplier partnership costs, not just your internal costs. Vendors who do all of the work to determine your inventory needs and generate corresponding Purchase Orders for themselves are not necessarily acting in the best interest of the partnership if significant expense is involved. Except under limited circumstances, it will be far more expensive for the vendor to travel to your site to determine inventory needs than to determine those needs with your own personnel.

It is important to understand all current methods that your organization uses to place PO's for consumable supplies, both formal and informal. Even if a department supervisor has the authority to contact a supplier and place an order without going through a formal purchasing process, that informal process is a part of your current practices and needs to be understood by the Lean TCO Program team. If that supplier will deliver to your facility without a formal PO issued by the Purchasing Department, that informal process must also be accounted for.

Procurement credit cards, or P-cards, provide the ability to purchase supply items without the expense of individual Purchase Orders. An employee, typically a buyer, who has been issued a P-Card has been given the authority to place orders for products without generating a Purchase Order and without going through the corresponding approval process. The accounting process is further simplified by the issuance of a single payment to the P-card provider rather than individual payments to each supplier. Recognize, though, that P-card processing costs can be extremely expensive for your suppliers (see Chapter 6).

Receiving

Receiving processes may seem simplistic and may appear to offer little opportunity for cost reduction, but the overhead costs associated with receiving activity can be substantial. Your Lean TCO Program team will need to review how shipments to your facility are verified, how they are moved into stocking locations, and how corresponding information is transmitted to your Purchasing and Accounting Departments.

If your receiving process causes measurable delay in getting supply items from your receiving dock to a stocking area, the corresponding costs can be substantial. I previously told the story of back-to-back orders we received from a customer for the same items due to their failure in getting the first delivery into their system. They did not know that the items they ordered a few days before were already at their facility, and they ordered those same items again. The value of the items was extremely low and the corresponding overhead costs for obtaining those items was a significant multiple of the order amount.

Improvement teams often need to challenge conventional thinking in order to help their organizations openly consider counter-intuitive ideas. Consider the following example exchange between a an improvement team member and someone in the Accounting Department:

Team Member: Tell me how you know what to pay our supply item vendors.

Accounting: We get packing lists from our Receiving Department that they have verified against vendor shipments. We match those packing lists to vendor invoices and run checks accordingly.

Team Member: Why do you need the packing lists?

Accounting: Well, we shouldn't pay an invoice if we don't have a packing list.

Team Member: OK, what does the packing list tell you?

Accounting: (Wondering how much the team member gets paid) It tells me what was received.

Team Member: Doesn't the invoice tell you that?

Accounting: (Now irritated) The invoice tells me what the vendor *claimed* they shipped, the packing list tells me what they *actually* shipped.

Team Member: So the vendors send invoices that don't agree with their packing lists?

Accounting: (Voice a little louder) No. Our receiving personnel tell us what was received and mark that on the packing list.

Team Member: So you're looking at what the receiving department said you received, not what the vendor said you received.

Accounting: (Trying not to sound condescending) Yes. Now you understand.

Team Member: What happens if the Receiving Department says the packing list was wrong?

Accounting: The packing list goes to the Purchasing Department so they can resolve it with the vendor.

Team Member: How often does that happen?

Accounting: I don't know. I only get packing lists that are ready to be matched to invoices.

Team Member: So what would happen if the Receiving Department didn't count all of the supply items in a shipment and just told you the shipment came in?

Accounting: (Now angry) Look, I'm a busy person and we've already covered this! We couldn't pay the invoice!

Team Member: I'm sorry, bear with me. What if you just paid the invoice?

Accounting: Then we could be paying for things we didn't receive!

Team Member: And that would be bad.

Accounting: (With a sigh) Yes, that would be bad.

The team member in this exchange may have been fairly shrewd and may have been asking some seemingly silly questions just to get the other person to think about why things are done the way they are. It is also possible that the team member really didn't understand the vendor payment process and just needed to get some answers. Either way, the exchanges between improvement team members and their coworkers often need to challenge conventional wisdom.

If the team member is not satisfied with the answers from the Accounting Department... not convinced that counting supply items when they are received is necessarily a good idea... their process analysis might continue with the Receiving and Purchasing Departments. They could determine whether or not the amount of time spent in counting supply items was significant, and they could also find out how often the Purchasing Department needed to resolve discrepancies with various suppliers. If inventory counting costs were high and discrepancies were infrequent, the team member could look at the cost of the discrepancies to compare the relative expense to the organization.

Perhaps the team member would determine that fasteners for the Maintenance Department were such a low cost item that counting the fasteners was highly unproductive. The improvement team might then recommend that fasteners received from the fastener supplier should go straight into inventory without being counted. They might draw the same conclusion for other low-cost item categories such as first aid supplies. To satisfy the reasonable concerns that the Accounting and Purchasing Departments might have, occasional random audits of incoming shipments could be arranged. Those audits might contractually allow compensation from the corresponding suppliers for past shipments if audits of current shipments reveal discrepancies.

Consider this from a strategic partnership perspective. If you are working strategically with a supplier to reduce costs incurred by both you and the supplier, it would be very reasonable to ask why the partnership should count supply inventory twice. I am not recommending that your Lean TCO Program team suggest that your organization stop verifying supply item shipments in your Receiving Department; this is just an example of how your Lean TCO Program team can dig into processes and challenge conventional wisdom.

Stocking and Distribution

Much like the supply chain, where we want to minimize costs associated with supply item movement within the channel, we also want to minimize supply item movement costs within your facility. Look at your stocking and distribution methods respect to the following:

1. The time required to get received supply items into known locations accessible by employees.

2. The time required for employees to access supply items.

I had an excellent opportunity to work with a customer in reducing costs associated with the internal movement of supply items. At this facility, a tool crib was used for storing safety, welding, and grinding consumables. This company had determined that excessive costs were being incurred due to the amount of time employees would spend obtaining items from the tool crib. They had already started an inventory organization effort and had appropriately determined that they needed to provide immediate supply item access to these employees. They had also determined that employees were spending too much time traveling from their work areas to the tool crib, and the decision was made to pursue some form of localized supply item access.

We implemented our Supply Control Systems software (visit www.LeanTCO.com for details) and assisted with the transition to distributed supply item access for production workers. The projected S2C savings for the overall Lean TCO Program was $761,000 on approximately $1,500,000 in annual spend. The following concerns needed to be addressed prior to implementing the distributed access solution:

1. The cost of a second supply inventory move from the tool crib to the access locations.

2. The method of controlling inventory levels within the access locations.

3. Security of the access location inventory.

Our Supply Control Systems software was implemented to manage tool crib inventory as well as inventory within the access locations. Weekly restocking intervals were chosen in order to minimize the manpower required to keep sufficient supply inventory in the cabinets. Similar to the desire to move large volumes of product within the supply chain whenever product movement is required, relatively large volumes of supply inventory would be moved at one time from the tool crib to the access locations. A tool crib attendant bringing a weekly supply of consumables to a production department is far more efficient than individual workers traveling to and from the tool crib to obtain individual items. This was also more productive for the tool crib attendant... they were now "handing out" one week worth of production department supplies at one time rather than a single supply item to a single employee at a time.

The access locations were lockable "open air" cabinets. The decision to use open air cabinets was based upon 5S visual principles; even if the cabinet was locked, a quick visual scan could confirm that supply inventory was available and that no unauthorized items were in the cabinet (a traditional lockable cabinet can quickly become filled with items that the cabinet was not intended for... everything from random tools to lunch boxes).

Regarding supply item security, this company decided to communicate to the production staff that the cabinets would be left unlocked during the production shift and that they would decide to lock the cabinets only if security concerns developed. The previous inventory security problems this company experienced were not due as much to shrinkage as to hoarding. The supply inventory was not being "stolen", it was being shuffled into worker toolboxes. The workers were experiencing frequent stock outs and tended to keep some excess supply in their toolboxes as a result. More hoarding would lead to more stock outs, and more stock outs would lead to more hoarding. Management communicated to the production staff that new inventory control methods were being implemented in the tool crib to help assure ongoing supply inventory availability and that hoarding would no longer be necessary. They also communicated that hoarding could lead to unnecessary stock outs for other workers.

(I learned a valuable lesson at this facility. Management respected the fact that workers hoarded supplies; they recognized that their employees would rather be able to work productively than stand in a line at a tool crib window. They took responsibility for the hoarding problem and solved the root cause of the problem... tool crib inventory control... rather than blaming the production staff.)

When looking at your internal supply movement, be certain to consider all costs associated with workers stocking and distributing items as well as costs associated with workers accessing those items. Your process improvements need to account for all supply item movement within your facility... from receiving activity to getting supply items into the hands of end users.

Accounting Transactions

Accounting transactions for consumable supplies go beyond processing invoices. Your organization's accounting system is likely to require transactions from the time product flows into your facility until the time payment for the product flows out. Depending upon the complexity of how supply items are tracked in your accounting system, there may also be *cost accounting* transactions when product moves within your facility.

When product is received, it is typically "posted" in the accounting system to show that the corresponding inventory is now on-hand and that the corresponding Purchase Order has been fulfilled. Most Accounting Departments will match the supplier's invoice to the supplier's packing list. The supplier can then be issued a check according to the terms on the supplier's invoice. If your organization tracks supply related costs by department or employee, there may be transactions that allocate supply costs accordingly.

It is the responsibility of the Lean TCO Program team to assess all accounting-related processes for value, efficiency, and effectiveness. Regarding value, do not assume that all accounting processes are necessary. P-cards are an example of a method to eliminate the majority of accounting transactions associated with supply items. The same is true for many Vendor Managed Inventory solutions. Needless to say, your organization has to have sufficient supply-related accounting activity to generate accurate financial statements regardless of any process changes that are implemented.

Accounting records can be a source of valuable information for your improvement team. Purchase Order frequency, Purchase Order amounts, backorders, rush delivery charges, restocking charges, and charges for services will be of great interest to your team members.

Chapter 10

Retaining and Furthering the Gains

All lean initiatives, your Lean TCO Program included, should conclude with the implementation of methods to secure the gains that have been achieved and to promote continuous improvement. For improvements to withstand the test of time, the underlying processes must be followed by all affected personnel. This is not just a matter of effective training, but ongoing follow-up that assures the process improvements are functioning as expected. Not only will this allow corrective action to be taken as necessary, follow-up activity will promote further improvements as opportunities arise.

Implement Written Procedures

The first step in securing process-related gains is to assure those processes are well documented. The process mapping work that the Lean TCO Program team has completed is the foundation for your written procedures. Your organization most likely has a formal Quality System that includes Operating Procedures and Work Instructions. I strongly recommend that all process documentation be included within your Quality System for the following reasons:

1. The documentation will follow a standardized and well understood structure.

2. Employees will be regularly trained according to the requirements of your Quality System.

3. Your Procedures and Work Instructions will be regularly audited for compliance according to the requirements of your Quality System.

Be certain that your documented processes include clearly assigned accountabilities. For any process to be effective, those ultimately responsible for the process must be identified. They are referred to as "Process Owners" in current Quality System language. Process Owners can help assure the successful launch of the process, can assist in monitoring the process, and can initiate quick corrective action if a process failure occurs. Process Owners can also be instrumental in assuring continuous improvement efforts are ongoing.

Assure that all affected employees are trained in their responsibilities. Communicate during the course of training how compliance to procedural requirements will help control costs. If your Lean TCO Program team has done a good job of promoting their work and gathering feedback, all affected employees should be ready and willing to support the new methods.

Don't Blame the Maverick Buyer

One of the first rules in identifying the root cause of a problem is to focus on processes rather than people. Although an employee may fail to follow procedure, most process problems can be traced back to process failures. Even employee performance issues can often be traced back to failures in employee training processes.

If a process failure occurs, determine what step (or steps) in the process were not performed properly and search for a process-related root cause. One of the most critical outcomes of your Lean TCO Program will be a standardized list of supply items, and one of the most damaging risks to that standardization is maverick buying. I will use maverick buying as an example of a process failure.

Although there are plenty of maverick buyers out there that disregard otherwise controlled supply procurement methods, the majority of the maverick buyers I have met would rather not have the title, let alone the role. How many people wake up in the morning with the desire to go into work and do some maverick buying?

> "When I get into the office I think I'll anger the folks in Purchasing by searching catalogs and buying something I know they wouldn't want me to buy. I really don't have anything better to do today than flipping through catalog pages anyways. Then I'll go buy some random item from a local store while I am out for lunch. That will really get them going."

I would argue that in the vast majority of cases, maverick buying occurs because someone has a need that is not being met by supply procurement and control methods.

> "Steve, thanks for getting that strapping tape for our shipping containers today. I can't believe we ran out again. We were able to ship on time thanks to you. Now follow me to HR. I've got to write you up for maverick buying. You really should have known better."

I may have again angered some readers, so let me say that I understand many maverick buying frustrations are legitimate. The issue of the control of maverick buying is just that... control. If maverick buying is occurring in your organization, could it be that management has not clearly communicated the excessive overhead costs that can result? Has your organization implemented a supply management system that assures the right supplies are always available when needed? With effective controls in place for specifying, procuring, and maintaining supply items, maverick buying temptations can be eliminated and those who continue to practice it can be more reasonably held accountable.

When implementing corrective action, don't confuse symptoms with causes and don't confuse personnel problems with process problems.

Continuous Improvement

One of the biggest challenges associated with consumable supplies is that supply items change frequently. Regardless of the level of success your Lean TCO Program team has in establishing a complete Supply Item Master List, that list will evolve over time. New production processes, new supply item alternatives, discontinued supply items, changes in suppliers, and changes in supply related processes can all impact the supply item list. Your objective is to assure the changes that occur will result in ongoing TCO reduction whenever possible.

Your organization should now view supply items much differently than before the launch of your Lean TCO Program. There should be an awareness of the substantial savings the team achieved and broad support of retaining those savings. Employees who would like to introduce a change in your Supply Item Master List should recognize how that change could impact TCO.

I advocate continuous improvement be driven by objectives that have been assigned to departments and/or individuals in your organization. Here are some sample objectives:

> "Consolidate the number of unique abrasives used in production by 10%."

"Evaluate competitive alternatives for spray chemicals and reduce annual spray chemical spend by 15%"

"Reduce receiving lead-time and assure all shipments are verified and placed into stocking locations within 1 hour of receipt."

"Identify the root causes of rush deliveries for supply items and reduce the number of rush deliveries by 25%."

With strategic supplier partnerships in place, your suppliers need to be involved in your internal cost reduction efforts and should also be offering their own suggestions for ways to reduce costs. Supply item alternatives and ideas for savings from within the supply chain should be brought to your attention on a regular basis.

I also advocate the use of employee suggestions as a means to identify further cost reduction opportunities. If your organization already gathers employee suggestions, be certain that employees know you are always looking for consumable supply TCO reduction ideas. If your organization does not already have a formal means for gathering employee suggestions, use your Lean TCO Program as a motivation to get one implemented. Your employees who use supply items are likely to be a valuable source of ongoing cost reduction opportunities.

Chapter 11

Multi-Facility Organizations

If you are reading this book as someone about to embark on an exciting journey to reduce consumable supply TCO across multiple locations, the savings that can result from a Lean TCO Program can be staggering... particularly if there has not been any successful prior effort to coordinate consumable supply specification and procurement between your facilities. As with any large scale accomplishment, the work ahead will be both highly challenging and highly rewarding.

There are two major obstacles in any multi-facility Lean TCO Program. The first obstacle is the challenge of integrating the individual needs and practices of each location. The degree of autonomy that each location currently enjoys will be directly proportional to the degree of effort required to achieve an integrated solution. The broader the array of needs and practices, the broader the array of measurement, analysis, and improvement activity. The second obstacle is the challenge of generating buy-in at each location. Many corporate level improvement efforts that simultaneously affect multiple facilities come down through the chain of command as corporate mandates. Many of those improvement efforts fail as a result. It is essential that the leadership of the Lean TCO Program not only show their respect to the affected employees at each location, but demonstrate that respect through a well coordinated effort of gathering, and acting on, feedback from those employees.

As with all improvement initiatives, successful implementation occurs only with the support and commitment of those tasked with carrying out the improvement effort. Problems can also arise when procurement professionals are mandated to purchase from a new source, and the full potential of this initiative will not be realized unless those procurement professionals share the vision of the initiative and develop confidence in any newly selected supplier's ability to outperform existing sources.

In some cases, buyers will have to let go of long-standing and trusted supplier relationships. Some of those relationships will have both professional and personal components. Although the buyer may comply with mandated sourcing requirements, the reasonable frustration they will experience may reduce a new supplier's ability to become a trusted partner. That, in turn, will limit what can be accomplished in ultimate TCO savings. Consideration must be given to how buyers will view the following in any new supplier:

- Knowledge and experience related to the commodities they provide

- Experience within the buyer's same industry

- The commitment to dependable product availability

- The effectiveness of the supplier's overall solution

By accounting for the legitimate concerns that buyers may have with respect to new sources, you can increase the likelihood of smoother transitions to those sources.

Building the Universal Supply Item Master List

Clearly, the significant opportunity for substantial savings in a multi-facility Lean TCO Program comes from the potential to dramatically reduce the number of unique supply items used across all locations. I have already discussed the challenge in consolidating supply items in a single facility; that challenge is increased many times over when multiple facilities are involved. It is not realistic to immediately begin building a master list of supply items for all facilities. Following the guidelines previously presented in this book, I recommend that each facility initiate their own standardization work and build their own supply item lists. Do not be concerned that this approach will cause wasted effort. Starting with facility-level standardization work will produce the following benefits:

1. A considerable reduction of the total number of supply items that must be addressed.

2. Greater supply item familiarity within each facility.

3. The ability to work with structured lists of supply items that include manufacturers and manufacturer part numbers.

4. The ability to readily compare supply item alternatives based upon individual facility experience.

As described in Chapter 2, the first step is to have each facility gain control of supply item selection. It will not be productive to have each facility working on standardization while new supply items are being introduced outside of controlled processes. The second step is to create a universal list of supply item categories that all facilities will use. Common category references will later facilitate the analysis of supply items across all locations; it will be much easier to coordinate multi-facility standardization work if all locations use the same item category terminology. Visit www.LeanTCO.com to learn about our online software that supports the use of universal supply item categories and universal supply item lists. With new supply item selection under control, and with universal supply item categories in place, you are now ready to launch the facility-level standardization effort.

The corporate-level Lean TCO Program team needs to maintain contact with each facility in order to follow progress and share information between facilities as appropriate. Generally speaking, I do not recommend trying to coordinate multi-facility supply evaluations due to the delays and disagreements that can result. The challenge will be great enough within each location, and once structure and standardization has been established at each facility, managing further evaluations across multiple facilities will be much easier.

Blending Local and National Suppliers

Do not assume that national suppliers must be used for all locations. You should anticipate that substantial savings will result from the consolidation of consumable supply procurement into fewer national sources, but remember the criticality of building strategic supplier partnerships. National sources with slightly better pricing may not be superior alternatives to local sources that know your operations and are prepared to forge strategic partnerships. I say that as a national supplier myself.

The primary consideration regarding local suppliers is not the potential for physical presence in your facilities. As a matter of fact, the physical presence of a supplier can be quite costly (see Chapter 5). The primary consideration is the working knowledge that local suppliers have with respect to your facilities. That working knowledge might include a combination of your processes, equipment, and personnel. If a supplier with the ability to form a strategic partnership exists at the local level, they should remain a candidate for your long-term sourcing needs.

When I was working in sales for our distribution business, I would often meet buyers that would express potential interest in doing business with us because of a frustration that they did not regularly see the salesperson with their current supplier. "Joe used to come buy at least once a month, but now that he has had our business for a while, I might not see him twice a year." Those kinds of comments were troubling to me on a number of levels. First, how could a supplier allow a valued customer to lose their sense of importance? Second, how was it that the customer's sense of importance became based upon the frequency of visits made by a salesman? Third, what exactly was the salesman accomplishing for the customer when they took the time to stop by the customer's location? Finally, is the buyer going to expect my physical presence in their facility in order to feel appreciated?

Here is what I have learned from these experiences. As I discuss at length in Chapter 6, we are relational creatures. Our sense of importance to another organization is only going to be developed by personal interactions with individuals that work for that organization. I travel frequently, and as a result, I have a number of what I call "plastic gold" relationships with a number of organizations. No matter how many plastic silver, gold, and platinum membership cards I receive in the mail, and no matter how many bonus points I am rewarded with, I don't feel appreciated by that organization until someone has a personal interaction with me as a valued customer. If it is a hotel, it might simply be the clerk behind the desk saying "thank you, we appreciate your business Mr. O'Meara" when they look at my "plastic gold" card as I am checking in. Even if they are just saying what they are trained to say, a personal "thank you" will always be more significant to me than 50,000 points on a printed form in an envelope.

Some of you are thinking "OK, you keep the verbal expression of gratitude and let me have your 50,000 bonus points." I get it. I know what it is like to trade in my bonus points for a new golf club. The issue is that we don't feel appreciated from impersonal interactions... the order and receipt of the new golf club made possible by those 50,000 points involved zero personal interaction. The hotel clerk handing me a little membership bag containing a free cookie and a bottle of water while saying "thank you" is far more likely to generate that internal sense of being appreciated than the "plastic gold" that comes in the mail.

Back to the buyer who misses his sales guy and how that relates to local sources of supply and potentially expensive supplier visits. There are better ways for suppliers to assure customers are appreciated than by traveling to the customer's location for face-to-face interaction. In the supply industry, there are many decades of traditional business practices between buyers and salespeople to overcome. One of those traditional practices is frequent meetings between buyers and salespeople that have no productive benefit for the buyer's organization. If you are reading this book as a member of executive management, ask yourself this question:

> *"Are the face-to-face relationships your buyers have*
> *with your supplier's salespeople an asset or a*
> *liability to your organization?"*

After thinking for a few moments, many will acknowledge that these in-person relationships can be *liabilities*. There are certainly times when a visit by a salesperson is appropriate, but they are few and far between. This is particularly true with today's technology.

We have many fantastic customer relationships with people we have never met. They know that they are appreciated because we provide personal service and personal attention... we just rarely provide it in person. They may receive an occasional electronic flyer or newsletter, but they also receive more personal emails and phone calls. Most importantly, they receive *service that demonstrates their value* to our company and to us as individuals.

Centralized Purchasing

Centralized purchasing of consumable supplies may or may not be appropriate for your organization. Consideration of centralized purchasing should occur within the Lean TCO Program and should not be a pre-conceived goal or expected outcome of your improvement efforts.

The potential benefits of centralized purchasing are clear:

- Control over indirect material spend
- Control over supply item specification
- Control over supply item sourcing
- Control over purchasing power

Consider government organizations. You may be reading this book as a government employee. Generally speaking, many would argue that government organizations have these two characteristics in common: *control and inefficiency.* Many citizens resent both the degree of control and the degree of inefficiency in the government organizations that serve them. I find that this same resentment often exists within corporations… employees at individual facilities can resent corporate-level control and corporate-level inefficiency.

I believe that this "emotional separation" between local facilities and corporate offices can occur in part due to the physical separation of corporate personnel from the day-to-day activities at their various locations. Even after the successful completion of your Lean TCO Program, consumable supply needs will place occasional urgent demands at each location. Like spending 2 hours of your day waiting to have your picture taken for a driver's license, an employee that can't get a job done due to a slow corporate-level response to a supply item need will generate both exasperation and resentment.

> "I am waiting for corporate to approve this new production tool. We can't continue manufacturing until they do. Worse yet, they're complaining about how we failed to plan for this tool and they want us to submit a Corrective Action."

If you are going to go down the path of centralized purchasing, be ready to head off the "Big Brother" concerns your facilities may have. Your supply related communication systems will need to be automated and readily available to all affected employees at each location. (Visit www.LeanTCO.com to learn about our multi-facility supply control solution.) Local buyers are first-hand witnesses to the sense of urgency when a sudden need arises. The VP of Operations may walk directly into the buyer's office to express the severity of a production delay. A buyer half-way across the country will need to have the same level of responsiveness as a local buyer that has had people in their office demanding immediate action.

Do not implement centralized purchasing for the sake of *control*. If you pursue centralized purchasing, do it for the sake of providing outstanding *service* to your individual facilities. Centralized purchasing can provide the opportunity to build a highly efficient and highly structured system of supply management services.

Your Lean TCO Program team must weigh the following factors if they consider a centralized purchasing solution:

1. Is there the potential for a high degree of item consolidation, or are the supply needs of the individual facilities largely unique?

2. What necessary services are local suppliers providing to the individual facilities?

3. Are there national suppliers that can provide necessary services to all facilities?

4. Is there substantial duplicated effort at the individual facilities that could be consolidated into corporate roles?

5. Is the potential value of multi-facility supplier consolidation mitigated by the value of strategic sources at the individual facilities?

6. Are the right resources available to implement a responsive, knowledgeable, and service-oriented centralized purchasing function?

The Lean TCO Program team needs to recognize that the price savings resulting from the buying power of centralized purchasing may be available even if purchasing activity remains distributed across individual facilities. Suppliers are often willing to negotiate volume price breaks based upon total usage rather than individual order size. Buyers are familiar with the term "last column pricing", where the "columns" represent item quantity price breaks or dollar volume price breaks. Suppliers may be willing to offer last column pricing, or even better, based upon expected annual usage alone.

I do not advocate centralized warehousing except under special circumstances. Remember our focus on reducing channel costs within the supply chain by reducing the number of times a product needs to be moved before arriving at a final destination. If you use centralized warehousing, you are inducing a second product shipment from the warehouse to your individual facility. Centralized warehousing may be logical when a sufficient number of relatively close locations require relatively small volumes of supply items. We are a supplier to a national corporation that provides construction services across the country. Their construction projects are generally large enough to justify onsite construction trailers used as temporary offices. We will ship small volumes of supplies to these individual locations, and we will also ship larger volume orders to a central location in the West. These larger volume orders are used to support construction projects in nearby states. This customer has determined that it is cost effective to use a combination of centralized and distributed supply item storage based upon project location.

Take Action

If you haven't already, get started. The challenge ahead of you is substantial. There will be a considerable amount of work required to implement the methods outlined here. Depending upon the size of your organization and the amount of manpower you can invest in your Lean TCO Program, you can expect to spend anywhere from a few weeks to many months on the project. If you need a little motivation, apply the following equation for a rough estimate of your Lean TCO savings potential:

$$\text{TCO Savings} = (1.5 \times \text{Annual Spend}) \times 0.25$$

A good rough estimate of typical overhead expenses is 50% of annual indirect material spend. Depending upon your current level of supply item control, savings could range from 20% to 50% of your current TCO. Using a conservative 25% savings estimate, the equation above yields a potential savings that is 37% of your current spend.

To develop a sense of urgency within your organization, divide 37% of your current annual spend by 12. Every month of delay is potentially costing your organization that amount of savings. For

$100,000 in annual spend, each month of delay represents over $3000 in savings that cannot be recovered. For $2,000,000 in annual spend, each month of delay represents over $60,000 in savings that cannot be recovered.

We offer seminars, on-site services, and online software to facilitate your Lean TCO Program. We also offer Lean TCO Certification for buyers, procurement consultants, lean consultants, and suppliers. Visit www.LeanTCO.com to sign up for our monthly newsletter and learn more about what we do.

Index

Jerry, thanks to you as well, timing is everything.